HOUDINI'S SCHOOL OF MAGIC

- VOLUME 1 -

Edited by
Leo Behnke

With additional Houdini material by
Geno Munari

Selective drawings by
Tina Verde

HOUDINI'S Magic Shop
Las Vegas, Nevada

Copyright 2009 by Geno Munari Publishing.
All rights reserved. No part of this publication may be reproduced or transmitted in any form or by any means, electronic or mechanical, including photocopy, recording, or any information storage or retrieval system, without permission in writing from the copyright owner.

ISBN: 978-1-61584-786-0

Printed in the United States of America

HOUDINI'S SCHOOL OF MAGIC

TABLE OF CONTENTS

Houdini's Life and Magic — 1
The Continent — 8
Back Home — 12
The Big Adventure — 13
His Greatest Sorrow — 13
Matinee Idol — 15
Challenging the Spirits — 16
Houdini's Magic — 18
Addressing the Audience — 18

Some History of Magic — 21
The Oldest Trick — 21
The Oldest Magic Name — 22
In the Renaissance — 23
Magic Showmen — 24
The New Breed — 26
The French Genius — 27
The Wizard of the North — 28
Professor Hoffmann — 29
Rabbits in Hats — 30
Golden Age of Magic — 31
Vaudeville Circuits — 32
Small-Time Acts — 33
Vaudeville Stars — 34
America's Illusionists — 35
World Travellers — 37
The Movies — 40
World War II — 41
Post War — 42
Television — 43
Mecca of Magic — 44

When You Do Magic 49
Preparation 50
Practice 51
Basic Rules 52
Movement 54
Timing 56
Personality 57
Learning More 58

Magic with Anything 61
Asbestos Handkerchief 61
The Ring Thing 62
Ghostly Glass 63
It's Matchic 64
Matchbook Mindreading 65
Pencil Penetration 65
Twice as Good 66
Spots or No Spots? 67
Straw Through 68
Odd or Even? 69
The Penetrating Matches 70
The Classic Coin and Glass 71
A Heavy Coin 72
Slide for Life 74
Catch It 75
13¢ of Mindreading 76
Interlude With a Knife 77
Beheaded Match 79
Moving Matches 80
Coffee Catch 81
Flying Ring 83
Which Way is Up? 84

Playing with Cards 87
Mechanic's Grip 87
The Spread 88
The Turnover Flourish 89
The Overhand Shuffle 89

The Hindu Shuffle	90
The Riffle Shuffle	91
Three Decks	92
The Selected Card	92
Piano Cards	93
Two Card Memory	94
All Follow Me	95
It Tells Me...	97
"Four Cards Down"	98
Three Pile Shuffle	99
Make Them Match	101
Riffle Impossibility	102
Slow-Motion Crooked Straight	104
Easy Does It	105
Spelling Mistake	106
Parachute Card	108
Pocket Challenge	108
"26"	110
Trick for a Beautiful Lady	112
Switch and Match	113
Three Card Monkey Business	114

Playing With Cards Some More — 119

Reversing a Card	120
Palming	122
The Double-Lift	123
Duplication	125
Here or Here?	126
Miraskill	127
The Spectator Finds It	128
Reverse Mistake	129
Elevator Cards	131
Process of Elimination	132
Up and Down	133

Money Magic — 135

Change of a Pencil	135
Quick Vanish	136

Fifty to One	137
It's That One	138
Coin Box	138
The Shrinking Quarter	140
A Fifth Pocket	141
Slow Nickel Vanish	142
Twenty-Five Cents	143
Right Through	144
Copper-Silver Through	145
Ten Penny Vanish	147
Digital Dollars	149
Two for Two	149
Dollar Change	151

One, Two, Magic! — 153

The Next Shape is...	153
1 to 9 Addition	154
What's the Meaning?	154
$1.15	154
3 Times 8 Equals 9	154
Eight 8s Equal 1,000	155
The Math Test	156
7x13=28	156
The Magic of 9	157
O T T F F S S E N	158
Three MAGIC Puzzles	158
Three in a Row	159
Square of Four	159
Square of Nine	160
A Different Version	160
Elimination	161
Magic Mnemonics	162
Playing Card Memory	164
Memorizing a Deck	165
Magic Squares	167
Sixteen-Cell Square	169
Balancing Water	171
Houdini Card	171
Houdini Card Uncovered	172

The Vanishing Coin	174
Egyptian Card Mystery	175
The Mystery Match	175
Making a Knot	176
Houdini's Shears	176
Through and Over	177
DeLand's Mind Reading Trick	178
The Afghan Bands	179
The Cups & Balls	180
Bibliography	**184**

HOUDINI'S SCHOOL OF MAGIC

HOUDINI'S LIFE AND MAGIC

The most famous magician in the history of conjuring wasn't as famous for his magic as he was for being the world's greatest escape artist, Harry Houdini. Although he spent his early career performing as a magician, he became more famous for the unbelievable situations he was able to escape from and his highly public battle to expose frauds. Houdini freed himself from not only simple bindings like chain shackles and numerous handcuffs, but also from more unusual predicaments like being sealed inside a large paper bag, locked inside a giant milk can filled with water, and hanging upside-down in a straitjacket fifteen floors above a busy street.

Born as Erik Weiss on 24 March 1874, in Budapest, Hungary, he came to the United States with his mother, three brothers, and a much older half-brother, to join their father in Appleton, Wisconsin, in 1876. His father, Mayer Samuel Weiss, came to the United States two years earlier and found work as a rabbi for a small Jewish congregation. Sad to say, he lasted only four years and had to move the family to Milwaukee. Not being able to find a congregation, he began doing odd jobs to earn enough money to support his large family.

During these hard years Ehrich, as he was now called, earned what money a boy could on the streets of a small city. It was then that he happened to see a show that featured a magician by the name of Dr. Lynn (1831-1899), whose real name was Hugh Simmons and whose feature trick he never forgot. It was called "Paligenesia" and in it Dr. Lynn cut off a leg, both arms, and finally the head of a man, and then fastened them back on so he could walk off stage. This started a strong interest in magic and later in life he would often comment about this fortunate beginning.

At the age of twelve he ran away from home and wandered for a time. Later, he and his father met in New York and put enough money together to bring the rest of the family from Milwaukee. His father had established a small congregation without a synagogue and Ehrich earned his share of income for the family by being a newspaper boy, telegram messenger, and performing other odd jobs. During this time he also pursued his two strong interests: one of athletic skills, and the other of learning more magic. He became a prize athlete in boxing, swimming, and running, winning several medals in various New York competitions.

He and a friend, Jacob Hyman, began delving into books about magic, saw magicians in the vaudeville theatres, and started performing simple magic shows around the neighborhoods. Ehrich and Jake called themselves "The Brothers Houdini," believing that by adding the letter "I" to the last name of a famous French magician (Jean Eugene Robert-Houdin) that it meant "like Houdin". Erich also started using the first name of Harry because it sounded more American and better with Houdini.

In 1891, at the age of seventeen, he left his steady job as a tie-cutter and went on the road with Jake. They appeared in dime museums and small theatres, getting farther and farther away from New York. In 1893, they found themselves working the Columbian Exposition, the World's Fair that was playing that year in Chicago. The great majority of their shows continued to be only one-night stands and Jake soon got discouraged. In 1894, Jake left the act and Harry's brother, Theo, became his new partner.

During this time he and Theo developed a simple trunk escape into a much better magic effect. This trick called Metamorphosis, had Harry tied inside a cloth bag, then put into a trunk that was locked and roped. He managed to change places with Theo in just three seconds while inside a draped framework. Harry then unlocked the trunk, removed the rope and revealed Theo inside the still-tied bag.

The new act didn't last long, though, as Harry met a singer on one of their shows. Her complete name was Wilhelmina Beatrice Rahner, known as Bess to everyone who met her. At the time she met the Houdini Brothers she was a singer and dancer with the Floral Sisters. Theo actually met her first, but she soon fell under Harry's spell and after three weeks, they were married and spent their honeymoon at Coney Island. From this point on, Harry and Bess worked the act together.

Because Bess was much smaller than Theo, about five feet tall and ninety pounds in weight as opposed to Theo's much taller and huskier body, she was much faster in the feature of the act, Metamorphosis. It was their best trick and they constantly improved upon it, performing it on special occasions even in the last few years of Harry's life.

HOUDINI'S LIFE AND MAGIC

Continuing to struggle in the poor conditions of small time show business, they worked dime museums, beer halls, and old small theatres. The beer halls were the worst venues as the audiences not only rowdy, but also didn't hesitate to yell out that they didn't like the act in front of them. The dime museums weren't much better. The only difference was that the audiences were more polite, but they did many more shows, anywhere from ten to fourteen every day. The situation was very much like a circus sideshow with two rows of high platforms on opposite sides of a large room. The acts worked for ten to fifteen minutes each in rotating order, right around the room to the exit. After the last act the audience left and a new one was brought in.

Bess was more accustomed to theatres and sometimes refused to work the museums, but Harry loved them. He spent all of his nonperforming time talking to the other acts and learning how each act was done. Soon he was also writing and untying knots with his toes, swallowing small eggs and regurgitating them, or even running pins under his flesh or through his cheeks. All of the acts, however, impressed on Harry that he had to have something to sell at the end of his spiel in order to make more money. This was the inspiration for his writing "The Adventures of a Versatile Artist", which he sold for many years in many editions, even when he was a successful vaudeville headliner.

They got a break by signing a contract with the Welsh Bros. Circus. In the following twenty-six weeks they did their magic act, a mind-reading act and a Punch & Judy show along with selling soap, and Harry played the wild man in the sideshow.

The next year they thought they had finally begun their way up the ladder of entertainment success when they signed on with a travelling burlesque show called "The American Gaiety Girls."

During the five months that the show managed to be booked through the eastern states, Harry not only began to perfect his skills of escaping from police handcuffs, but he was also learning the value of publicity outside of the theatre's normal advertising. On the show's first day in a town, he would visit the local police station with a reporter and challenge the police to put handcuffs on him so he couldn't escape. With very few exceptions, he did escape, often in a very short time. Along the way he added the feature of being handcuffed and then locked inside a jail cell from which he would escape.

Unfortunately, the road show finally closed and the Houdini act joined another magician, Marco, to continue on through the northeastern states and into eastern Canada. Again, an absconding manager stranded them, but Harry had added another important escape to his repertoire. In St. John, New Brunswick, he had seen a mental patient strapped inside a straitjacket. After watching the man fight the jacket until he was exhausted, Harry's imagination was fired and he borrowed a jacket to practice in. Finally, he did the escape in public, was successful, and now had another very impressive act.

Houdini wasn't the only one presenting an act based on escapes, as there were also Brindamour and Vancos, who both did handcuff and trunk escapes, and the Great Raymond (1877-1948), who went on to become another world-touring headliner. The trunk escape wasn't that much of an exclusive as Englishman John Neville Maskelyne (1839-1917) first did it in 1865. He even featured it when he was booked for an engagement at Britain's famous Crystal Palace in 1869. There's no record of how the secret of the trunk trick traveled from England to the United States, or how Harry happened to learn it. But it did fit his style, and he performed many versions of it from his teenage years until a year or so before his death.

Harry was the only one however, who did an escape from a straitjacket. He also challenged his audiences and the local police departments to use any of their own handcuffs on him. These differences weren't enough to make him stand out from the others.

Near the end of 1897, they went back on the road by joining Dr. Thomas Hill's unit of the California Concert Company, a company that sponsored various medicine shows. Each unit would travel in a certain part of the country (Dr. Hill's territory was in the midwestern states) with a group of three to six entertainers. They would do a free show on the street, on an outdoor stage, or in a rented tent, to bring in the crowd and then Dr. Hill would pitch his "medicine." Things were better now as they were paid twenty-five dollars a week plus board and travelling expenses, with Bess singing and Harry playing a tambourine and doing his magic. They also experimented by trying new tricks and acts, including a spiritualist period where they supposedly produced the spirits of departed relatives for members of their audiences. These hoaxes weren't the same as doing magic tricks, but it allowed them to send some money home and still have a little left in their pockets.

The job lasted for almost four months but the medicine show finally folded and they were again forced to work in the Welsh Bros. Circus. Now, at least, Harry was able to do his larger magic effects, like Metamorphosis, and to larger audiences. Again, each one of them did a variety of acts to earn their three square meals a day, with Harry doing three different magic routines. He offered to do the handcuff escapes for another five dollars a week, but was refused by the manager. By the time the circus closed for the winter, they were doing Metamorphosis as the closing act of the circus performance. This provided them with a very good letter of recommendation from the circus management saying that Metamorphosis was "the strongest drawing card of its class in America."

Harry and Bess returned to New York where they started to restructure the act and make up new costumes for the 1898 season. Also, using his mother's house as a mailing address, he started the first of two schools, "Professor Harry Houdini's School of Magic". He printed flyers that asked, "Do you want to learn an act?" and followed that with a small sixteen-page catalog. The catalog was filled with descriptions of some magic apparatus that was provided by Roterberg of Chicago. It mostly offered secrets he had learned as he traveled about the country doing magic, not only the secrets of magic tricks, but also the real secrets of some of the acts that had worked on the same circus and museum bills with him. He offered to teach anyone how to swallow needles and thread them on a length of thread, how to eat fire, and how to have rocks broken on their chest, as well as how to operate a Punch & Judy show or do simple escapes.

The following spring they went back on the road to play some dates that they were contracted for and to see if they could find new places to perform the act. In a beer hall in St. Paul, Minnesota, they finally played the right act to the right people.

A party of theatrical managers dropped in to see the show. Among them was a man named Martin Beck. The show included Harry's challenge to escape from handcuffs and the next day Beck brought some to put on the bragging magician. Harry knew what he was talking about, however, and he escaped with ease. Martin Beck went back to his theatrical booking office and a few days later he wired the Houdinis. The wire read, "You can open Omaha March twenty-sixth, sixty dollars, will see act probably make you proposition for all next season." Houdini kept the telegram for the rest of his life, writing across the bottom, "This wire changed my whole Life's journey."

It certainly did. Not only did Harry and Bess start making double their salary, but they were also now playing legitimate theatres every week. They went from playing as many as fourteen shows a day in dime museums, to only two a day in front of comfortably seated audiences, and they now stayed at a theatre for at least a full week.

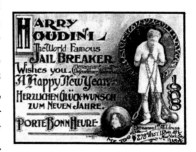

HOUDINI'S SCHOOL OF MAGIC

In just a little over a year they became a good, dependable vaudeville act. Martin Beck was one of the founders of the Orpheum vaudeville circuit and was very smart about operating in show business, as he had worked himself up through the ranks of actor, manager, waiter, prop man and many other of the lesser jobs in show business. At the time that he hired the Houdinis, his Orpheum circuit covered theatres in the entire western United States and he could book an act for a year without repeating the act in any theatre or any city. By the 1920s, the agreement between Beck's Orpheum circuit and B.F. Keith's United Booking Office controlled all the theatres in the entire country. Beck always booked good acts, paid the best salaries, and provided good, clean theatres for the performers and the audiences. Houdini's contract with Martin Beck took him to the leading theatres throughout the western half of the United States, including San Francisco, Los Angeles, and Denver. It was Denver where Houdini made a publicity splash. He wasn't yet a headliner, he was still just a supporting act, but Beck kept encouraging him and giving him basic advice, and Houdini kept learning more and more about his craft of escaping from anything. He was doing less magic and more escapes in the act, and their salary kept increasing.

Probably the biggest reason he was getting these fabulous raises in money in such a short period of time was that he generated a lot of publicity outside the theatre. He created big newspaper headlines and stories by escaping from jail cells in police stations. He was also escaping from custom locks and irons made by mechanics in every city he visited and many times he invited the public to see the result of a challenge on the stage of the local Orpheum theatre. When the people went in to see Houdini, they would naturally increase the box office receipts of that theatre regardless of which headliner was on that week. Therefore, Houdini brought in much more than his share of the receipts for Beck's theatres. Beck not only got his fifteen-percent commission of Houdini's weekly salary because he was his booking agent, but he also got an increased income from his share of that theatre's weekly profits of ticket sales.

In addition to the challengers to Houdini's mechanical knowledge, many local merchants tied their businesses in with Houdini by comparing their products or services with the escape artist's name. Their advertisements kept the Houdini name in front of the public, so that his fame grew. Finally, in May of 1899, he had his picture in the papers for the first time (a cartoon, actually), and he ran to their hotel room to show Bess. "Bess," he yelled, "We're made! I'm famous!"

HOUDINI'S LIFE AND MAGIC

In October of 1899 the Orpheum contract ended and, after a disagreement with Beck, the Houdinis had to start booking their own shows again. The B.F. Keith booking office wouldn't book him on a continuous tour, but made him work a grinding and nerve-wracking week by week, theatre by theatre. His previous publicity helped to get the dates and his continuing ability to garner more publicity kept the dates coming. He was famous, he was successful in besting his challengers, but he wasn't a headliner and the local offices wouldn't give him the dates he wanted. He needed to make a change.

In May 1900, Houdini and Bess sailed for England on the SS *Kensington*. He arrived with very little money in his pockets, and also without any bookings. An international agent, Richard Pitrot, had assured Houdini that there would be contracts, not only for England but also for Paris and Berlin as well. But when Houdini arrived in London he found that he not only didn't have any contracts, but that he was a stranger as well. His only hope was a written introduction from one of the passengers aboard the ship. The man liked the magic Houdini had performed during the various shows on the ship, and he wrote a note to C. Dundas Slater, the manager of the Alhambra Theatre.

The Alhambra was only one of about five hundred theatres in and around London, but Slater was always willing to look at something different for his customers. Slater booked a special performance for Houdini on a Wednesday afternoon, and invited other theatre managers and some newspaper reporters to see what this brash American could do. At Houdini's request there were also some men from Scotland Yard.

Houdini and Bess presented their basic vaudeville routine of a few card tricks, the substitution trunk, and the best of his escapes from handcuffs and chains. The only thing different was that he didn't do his escapes inside a cloth cabinet but behind a three-fold screen, and he did them as fast as possible.

Well, they hadn't seen anything like it. Houdini was immediately booked for the first two weeks of July at the Alhambra, but was held over for an additional six weeks. He then set out on a tour of the provinces and the smaller cities in England. His performances were great successes, but when he tried to challenge the various police departments into letting him escape from their jails, he met with great resistance. Most of the officers in charge didn't want their jails ridiculed if Houdini made good on his boast. Not being able to publicly escape from many British jails, he then recreated a jail escape on the stages of the theatres. He was handcuffed, put into a barrel, which was chained and padlocked, and it was rolled into a small cubicle decorated as a jail cell. A cloth was draped around the cell, and after a minute, it was rolled out again and unlocked. When the lid was removed, there was Bess, who had been onstage just a few moments before. Houdini then walked on stage from the wings.

At this point Houdini began to utilize some of the ideas he'd been thinking about for years. One of them became a standard for both escape artists and magicians even until today, and that was escaping from a packing box made by local carpenters. The box would be made, exhibited in the lobby before the performance, and then brought onstage at the appropriate time. Houdini would get inside, the lid would be nailed on, and the box roped or chained as a further difficulty. Houdini, however, would always walk out from his cloth cabinet a minute or two later, and the box would still be nailed shut and tightly roped. Even though the trick where Houdini and Bess changed places inside a locked trunk was a good trick, the packing box was even better. It used an item made out of everyday wood and not a trunk carried by the magician, it was made by people who wanted to challenge Houdini, and it also gave the local company that made the box some publicity. Houdini's challenges to the public started bringing more serious challengers and bigger publicity. Many times the challenge was so difficult that Houdini might hold up the show from fifteen minutes to an hour and a half, but the audiences waited for him. And when he finally did appear, free of all restraints, he was wildly cheered and treated as a hero. The press loved him and was very quick to point out that one man was challenging the best of England, and winning.

Houdini was considerably more sure of himself now, and he began writing Martin Beck about being released from the remainder of his contract. He calculated how much he owed Beck on his foreign contracts so far, and offered even more to be released. The escape king was again successful because after more negotiations about the final price, Houdini paid five hundred dollars to escape his contract, and immediately started forgetting about Martin Beck, the man who opened the bigger and better doors for him.

THE CONTINENT

After playing through western England and up into Scotland, Houdini launched a one-man campaign on the continent of Europe. He played the biggest theatres and circuses in France and Germany, as well as many of the other cities. Along the way he also began eliminating many of the competing performers who were also escaping from handcuffs and chains. One of these, Kleppini, was working the Circus Sidoli in Dortmund. Although Houdini was working in Holland at the same time, he heard that Kleppini was announcing that he had defeated Houdini in a handcuff competition. Catching a train to Dortmund, Houdini disguised himself (the first of many, many times) and attended the Circus Sidoli. When Kleppini again made his announcement, Houdini leaped into the ring, tore off his false mustache, and called Kleppini a liar. He also offered five thousand marks if Kleppini successfully escaped from a pair of Houdini's handcuffs, and he also offered to escape from Kleppini's feature trick, the "Chinese Pillory."

The cuffs Houdini was offering were a pair of French letter cuffs, the lock being a five-dial combination lock with letters that had to be aligned in a certain order for the cuffs to open. Houdini demonstrated them for Kleppini's manager, and then went out to put them on Kleppini. After thirty minutes in his cabinet, Kleppini was bypassed and the rest of the show was presented. He was still in trouble when the show ended, and, finally, at one o'clock in the morning he emerged and admitted defeat. Houdini then turned the dials to spell F-R-A-U-D to open the cuffs, not the word C-L-E-F-S (the French word for "key") that he had shown Kleppini's manager. While walking from backstage to the circus ring, Houdini had changed the combination. Houdini not only successfully eliminated most of his competition, but also realized that there was big business in the field of escapes; that is, more business than he could handle by himself. So he sent a telegram to Hardeen, his brother back in New York, and had him come to Europe and bring all the escape equipment he could find. They played in competition with each other, many times in the same city, and had great fun when they got together out of the sight of the public and compared notes about their shows and challenges.

Houdini kept jumping back and forth from England to the continent, seemingly to give meaning to his new nickname, "The Elusive American." He'd play a few months in the provinces of England, and then go to France or Germany, his two best countries for audiences. Before working in Germany for the first time, however, he had to be examined by the police. Every performer had to sit down and write a complete explanation of what they did when they were on the stage, and the police would then delete the parts of the act that they didn't like. Germany was a very authoritarian country as opposed to most of the rest of Europe, and the police had almost as much power as the police of Russia did.

Finally, he appeared before the police board in the new police headquarters in Berlin. He was stripped naked, his arms tightly clamped behind him, finger locks applied, and five different types of elbow irons and handcuffs. With his mouth bandaged and working under a blanket, he escaped in six minutes while being watched by 300 policemen. For this work he received an ambiguous statement, but he was free to work in Germany.

The following year, while again working in Germany, a newspaper wrote an article that accused Houdini of trying to bribe a policeman. Houdini immediately hired a German lawyer and sued both the newspaper and the policeman.

After many delays the trial began in Cologne in February of 1902, and ran for two days. Each of the two accused parties gave their versions of the events in question, and then another twenty-five witnesses took the stand to support the previous testimony. Finally, Houdini opened one of the locks in question in full view of the court and had himself locked in chains. Taking just the judge into one of the corners of the courtroom, Houdini let him see just how he effected his escape, and the verdict was in favor of Houdini. Both the policeman and the newspaper were ordered to pay damages to Houdini (very small ones, though), and the newspaper also had to print a retraction.

The resultant publicity filled German newspapers from border to border, and Houdini again brought in huge crowds to the theatres and earned more money.

The problem wasn't over, however, as the policeman appealed the verdict. The following July saw a second trial, but Houdini again opened a lock that the cop said he couldn't open, and again he won. This time, however, the fines on the policeman were enormous, and Houdini reaped more publicity. He had special posters made that showed him in front of a German judge and text that described the result of the trial. With the feelings of the public secretly against the oppressive methods of the police, Houdini had no trouble gathering more publicity.

While working in Paris, a Russian theatrical agent saw Houdini work and booked him for Moscow in 1903. Other events prolonged the bookings in Russia, but he couldn't wait to finally leave that country.

Leaving Berlin on 2 May, Houdini took a train to Russia, but the trip had unforeseen complications. At the Russian border the guards took away his passport, his books, and all of the newspapers he had with him. They completely searched his baggage, and were going to keep the trunk that held his desk, typewriter, correspondence, and other materials. They said a censor would inspect it, but Houdini didn't take the chance and had it shipped back to Berlin. He then had to pay exorbitant fees that were called custom duties, but they were levied against props that he'd been carrying for years, certainly not new merchandise.

When he arrived in Moscow he found that the police could also stop any performance they wanted, and could deport you and make you leave Russia within twenty-four hours. In addition, the performers had to buy large quantities of expensive tax stamps to put on their contracts in order to collect their salaries.

In spite of all this, or possibly because of it, one of Houdini's greatest challenges came about. It wasn't just with a lock or two, but with the penal system of Russia. He challenged the Russian secret service to lock him inside one of the metal vans that transported prisoners from place to place. Unknown to the police, Houdini had secretly looked into one of the vans when it had been parked to water its horses, and he was sure he could do the job.

When the police and Houdini met, they not only put him in handcuffs and leg irons, but also stripped him and gave him three complete physical searches before locking him in the van. He started to work, and twenty minutes later he opened the door, closed it, locked it again, and walked over to reclaim his clothes. The police not only searched him again, but also searched his assistant who came with Houdini to the jailyard.

Even though it was a daring action for a foreigner to take, because the secret police had absolute power over everyone, Houdini knew it was newsworthy. Except, he not only didn't get any newspaper publicity, but the police also refused to give him a promised certificate about the escape.

When he returned to Germany he again had posters printed, this time showing him defeating the Russian police force.

He continued to play in Russia for five months, but was constantly on watch for police spies and tricks that the police might pull in order to deport him. Being Jewish, he was also very aware of the anti-Semitism in the country. The Jews were attacked on the streets and in the press, and while he was there the pogroms killed many. Jews were not allowed in Moscow, reserving that rich but backward city for Russians only. After another long search at the border, Houdini and Bess with their assistant, Franz Kukol, were finally allowed to leave Russia.

Houdini spent another two years in Europe, constantly gathering newspaper publicity, creating large crowds wherever he played, and increasing his salary. When he started in England he was being paid $300 a week, and when he left for America it had jumped to $1,000. One week he even made $2,150, the highest he was to ever achieve, even though in his last years he was earning close to that amount as a continuing weekly salary.

"Pretty good," he wrote in his diary, "for Dime Museum Houdini."

BACK HOME

Arriving in New York in September of 1905, Houdini immediately got in contact with all the agents and managers he knew and started another vaudeville tour. He also began a series of sensational publicity stunts to advertise his appearances at the local theatres. In Washington, D.C., he escaped from the cell that had held Charles J. Guiteau, President Garfield's assassin. Houdini not only escaped from that cell, but also mixed up the other prisoners into the wrong cells, and stole his clothes out of another locked cell. He walked into the warden's office twenty-seven minutes after being locked up.

Later that winter he did the first of his bridge jumps. Jumping from a bridge into a river or bay while handcuffed and usually with leg irons as well. The most publicized of his jumps was the one where he jumped into the Detroit River in the middle of winter, the river covered with a solid sheet of ice. He was, supposedly, lost when he came back to the surface and couldn't find the hole he jumped through. After an extraordinary length of time, during which he used bubbles of trapped air under the ice to replace his exhausted air, he finally found the hole and emerged. Actually the jump took place when the river wasn't iced over, so the account must have been blown up by Houdini's active imagination.

Through the years, however, Houdini successfully did the bridge jump in bays on both coasts and in most of the major rivers in between. It was a sure publicity stunt, especially when he ran into difficulty with the local police. When he thought that the police might try to stop him, he would sometimes advertise that the jump would be from a certain bridge. He actually showed up at the next bridge down the river after a big word-of-mouth campaign to make sure the public was at the right bridge.

One of his ideas, which he performed for many years, was his Milk Can. He had an oversized can, which looked like the milk cans of farmers and dairies and big enough for him to get into. It was filled with water, and Houdini, properly handcuffed, slid down into the water, and they locked the lid over him. After a couple of minutes inside the cloth cabinet, Houdini emerged, wet but triumphant. After five years of successfully working in Europe, Hardeen also returned to America, again at Houdini's call, and the challenges continued.

Through the years Houdini escaped from giant envelopes, glass bottles, beer barrels, a huge football, and many mailbags provided by the local post office. Other restraints included automobile snow chains, rattan laundry hampers, and even a Witch's Chair, that had been used to dunk witches during the early days in New England.

THE BIG ADVENTURE

Besides being a daredevil at heart, Houdini couldn't pass up an opportunity to gather additional newspaper publicity. In 1909, while playing again in Germany, he bought a Voisin biplane and learned how to fly. He had it crated and carried it with him when he journeyed to Australia. He not only knew that no one had flown a plane in Australia yet, but that there were a couple of other men who were planning to do so.

He established a base at Digger's Rest, about twenty miles outside of Melbourne where he was playing. During a month of commuting between the theatre and the flying field he managed to make some flights, but all were minor disasters, mostly because of the winds. Then on March 18, 1910, he flew three times, the last time meeting the requirements of the international flying association. Just to make sure, he also flew on the 19th and the 20th, the last day's flight covered six miles and lasted seven minutes and thirty-seven seconds at an altitude of a hundred feet, battling winds all the way.

He also flew in Sydney during the next two months, barely averting disasters. In a joyous ceremony at the Sydney Town Hall the Australian Aerial League awarded Houdini a trophy as the first man to fly in Australia.

HIS GREATEST SORROW

On the seventh of July, 1913, Houdini and Bess boarded the *Kronprinzessin Cecilie*, a ship of the great North German Lloyd shipping company. His mother, named Cecilia, like the ship, and part of his family came to the dock to see them off. Houdini was not only booked to give a command performance for the king of Sweden, but he also planned to visit Budapest, the city where he was born. He was going

HOUDINI'S SCHOOL OF MAGIC

to appear under his legal name as he had petitioned the courts and changed it from Erich Weiss to Harry Houdini.

In Copenhagen there were two telegrams waiting for Houdini, one each from two of his brothers, Leopold and Hardeen. Both of them carried the news that his mother had been paralyzed by a stroke and was in critical condition. Houdini immediately cancelled his shows and jumped onto a ship to take him home. He arrived too late to see his mother alive, but was able to sit with her before she was buried, against all Jewish laws, which called for burial within a day of a death. After sitting up with her body, he placed inside the casket a pair of slippers he had bought for her in Germany, her last request when he had left her. She was buried in Machpelah cemetery in Queens, next to her husband and Houdini's half-brother.

He stayed home for the next several weeks brooding over his loss and visiting her at the cemetery. Even as close as he had been to his mother during her lifetime, he became even more so after her death. He filled a number of scrapbooks, letters, and conversations with references to her, and collected poems about mother love and devotion. His desire to be with her once again was the catalyst that later lead to his denunciation of so many fake spiritualists. He wanted to believe that he might be able to once again communicate with her, but found that all the seances he attended were frauds. All the rest of his life he never lost hope that someone might be able to show him how to once again talk with his beloved mother.

In 1877 two brothers, Antonio and Francis Martinka, had opened a magic shop in New York, located at 493 Sixth Avenue. They were experienced in creating, making, and providing magic for magicians as they had been in the same business in Vienna, Berlin and New York before they opened this particular shop. Their shop prospered and they were at that address for the next forty years, making both their apparatus and name famous around the world.

Antonio Martinka died in 1915, and Francis continued on for another two years before he decided to retire from the cold and snow of New York. Charles Carter, known on stages around the world as Carter the Great, decided that he'd like to own a magic shop as it fit right in with his being the "greatest magician in the world", so he bought it. What he hadn't figured on was that it's very difficult to run a shop in New York when you're performing shows in China or Australia. So, in 1919 he started looking for a new owner.

Houdini had just finished starring in a silent film named *The Grim Game*, in which he played a modern hero who gets into and

HOUDINI'S LIFE AND MAGIC

out of one dangerous situation after another, and he performed almost all of the dangerous feats in the film in person. Since he'd been paid $2,500 a week for making the film, he decided that he could use the extra money to buy Martinka's Magic. So he did.

Using the usual Houdini flair for publicity, he put ads in the magic magazines and printed some catalogs that had his name scattered all through the text. But after nine months, even Houdini could see that the shop, for some reason, wasn't going to be as successful as Houdini himself. He sold the shop to Otto Hornmann, who already had a New York magic emporium, and Hornmann combined the two businesses. It continued on through the years, moving to other addresses twice, and just recently closed, after 125 years.

MATINEE IDOL

After *The Grim Game*, Houdini went on to star in another film, titled *Terror Island*. Again, he played a hero who is continually captured by the bad guys and tied up, chained up, boxed up, or generally incapacitated by the ruffians. At the beginning of the following Saturday's matinee, however, audiences saw Houdini wriggle out of his predicament and continue on toward the final reel.

Terror Island, filmed mostly on Catalina Island off the coast of Los Angeles, was not a raving success, and Jesse Lasky, the producer, did not renew Houdini's contract. Houdini, in typical fashion, decided that he didn't need the established studios of early Hollywood to hire him for starring roles, he'd create his own motion picture company.

Mystery Pictures Corporation had Houdini as president and Hardeen (his escape artist brother) as vice-president. Unfortunately, their first film was made up of stock footage of Egypt and based on an Italian film that he bought at auction, titled *The Ashes of Passion*, all copies of which were lost over the years. His next feature, *Man From Beyond*, was about a prehistoric man who was chopped out of a chunk of ice and brought into the modern times of 1921. To get as much publicity as possible, Houdini teamed the movie with a short stage show, hoping that his name as a live performer would improve the size of the audiences. Word of mouth, however, made the film just another movie, and it didn't become the great success Houdini expected.

In his drive for celebrity, Houdini had at one time also put out his own magazine for magicians only and filled it with his articles and editorials. The first issue was published in September 1906 and was titled *Conjurers' Monthly Magazine*. Houdini had strong opinions about everything and everyone and in no time at all he was in a printed feud with Dr. A.M. Wilson who published the *Sphinx Magazine*, a longstanding and respected periodical for magicians. Finally, because of so many projects taking him in different directions, Houdini stopped publication and the August 1908 copy was the last issue.

So, again, Houdini put all of his energy into personally doing everything for his next film, *Haldane of the Secret Service*, which he produced in 1923. He wrote it, directed most of it, and even filmed some of the scenes himself in Europe. The film was released, but the reviewers and audiences agreed that it wasn't that good. With four different companies involved in the film business, his growing battle with fake spiritualists who bilked the grieving families of World War I soldiers, and the books he was working on, let alone the shows and personal appearances that he made, Houdini was in a constant whirlwind. After reading the reviews and seeing the box office receipts for this film, he made sure that it was his last film, and he closed all of his movie companies.

CHALLENGING THE SPIRITS

All during his performing life Houdini had challenged other people. He asked them to tie him up, drape him in chains, drop him in a river, or seal him in any container, and he said he would not only answer the challenge but beat it as well. Now, however, he was on a new tack. Now he was challenging the spiritualists who were supposedly bringing messages from the spirits of deceased friends and relatives, and then promising that those spirits could guide the living relatives on courses that would make the spirits happy. This usually involved the investment of money in some building dedicated to the memory of the departed one, or as a simple gift to the spiritualist medium because he or she was doing such good work for the spiritual world.

Houdini didn't see it that way. When he attended a seance to see how the spirits acted and communicated with the live sitters around the seance table, he saw fakery, and usually not very good fakery at that. Because of the love and devotion for his departed mother, this situation hit Houdini very hard. In a number of cases he followed up on what happened after the seances and found that all sorts of problems happened to the innocent contributors to the racket. Many of those victims became morose and disappointed because they could no longer contact their loved ones after the money ran out, and a few actually became suicides because of their despair.

Using his sharply honed sense of publicity, a group of dedicated assistants who attended seances and gathered information, and a series of lectures and demonstrations that showed exactly how the mediums duped their customers, Houdini went after the growing racket. As far as Houdini's notes, letters to friends, and remembered conversations can be researched, Houdini was never against the hope that the living might be able to contact the dead in some manner. But he was against the fake mediums who used simple tricks in the dark in order to line their own pockets, or, even sadder, just for the notoriety.

After his assistants gathered information by sitting in seances under assumed names, or even after Houdini had disguised himself and went to a seance in person, he started showing his theatre audiences how the fake mediums worked. At first, he did two or three demonstrations during his show, but then he began to do special lectures and demonstrations where an entire hour or two was devoted to writing on sealed slates, ringing bells, and making spirit voices.

He would invite two or three members of the audience onto the stage, blindfold them so they could not see, and then conduct a typical seance. The audience could see exactly what Houdini was doing while playing the role of the medium, but each of the blindfolded members was completely baffled.

Naturally, the spiritualists were up in arms as many of them were sincere in their beliefs, and they thought that Houdini was attacking the entire corps of spiritualist congregations. His audiences always held a number of shouting people who vilified Houdini personally, as well as telling everyone that he was a fake himself. But he was successful in his drive, and in city after city he exposed the fakers and got them prison sentences and fines. Many went out of business after Houdini was through working in their town.

But the big finish didn't happen for Houdini. One of the many committees in Congress was debating a bill in a committee that was aimed at the fraudulent business of spiritualism, and he was strongly in favor of regulating the medium trade. Finally, in early 1926, they called on Houdini to testify and demonstrate. During the four days of presenting what he felt was convincing evidence and displays of fakery, Houdini made headlines across the nation and drew more condemnation from honest believers. The committee, however, couldn't work out a way to word a bill to prevent fake mediums without crossing the lines that frame the First Amendment. They didn't recommend the bill to Congress, and Houdini was disappointed that the public had lost a weapon in the fight against the con men and women who preyed on honest people who wanted some consolation after a great loss. But he continued in his crusade right up to his death.

HOUDINI'S MAGIC

To bolster his image as a great magician, as well as to get any kind of publicity, Houdini had a lot of magic printed under his name. Some of it he wrote, and reporters and ghostwriters wrote some for him. The subjects of his writing ran from simple magic for beginners ("Red Magic" in the *New York World*) to thick books that required years of research and work (*A Magician Among the Spirits*, Harper and Bros.), but all were saleable because of the Houdini name.

But before we explain some of the magic that Houdini wrote about, let's give you some of his views on performing magic.

ADDRESSING THE AUDIENCE
An Editorial by Houdini

"The great trouble with magicians is the fact that they believe when they have bought a certain trick or piece of apparatus, and know the method of procedure, that they are full-fledged mystifiers.

The fact really is, it is not the trick itself, nor is it the mere handling of it. A successful presentation depends on the address in connection with the presentation.

When an artist, even a magician, is corrected by a critic, he should not be dismayed, nor should he look upon it as wasted. He should consider it a friendly favor and look upon it as I have always looked upon criticism.

When you introduce an experiment, apply yourself seriously. Don't think that because you perform a trick well or the apparatus is detection proof from the viewpoint of an ordinary audience, that you have conquered the world of mystery and that you reign supreme. Work with determination that you intend to make them *believe* what you say. Say it as if you mean it, and believe it yourself. If you *believe* your own claim to miracle doing and are sincere in your work, you are bound to succeed.

The reason magicians do not forge to the front more than they now do, is that they content themselves with mere doing and imagine they have the act complete; that all they have to do is to lay the apparatus on the table and go from one trick to the other. The experiment and apparatus are both of secondary consideration. Your determination to improve the seriousness of your endeavors means success, and if you are a natural comedian (I do not mean a buffoon or something which does not become your personality), you may easily inject a tinge of humor into your work. But do not strain that point; it should come naturally and with ease.

Herrmann's method with an audience was: As soon as he appeared to their gaze, he bowed and smiled, and bowed and smiled all the way to the footlights as if he were tickled to death to have the honor of appearing before them, and the effect on his audience was salutary, and he won their sympathy forthwith.

Dean Harry Kellar's method was to walk in just the same as he would into a house party, welcoming all. He knew he was presenting a line of feats that the majority present might have known, but he handled each number beautifully, and he knew that the audience loved to see him do it. Therefore, everything he presented inspired the audience to a feeling of kindliness toward him, and an appreciation of his work."

On October 24, 1926 Houdini arrived at the Garrick theater in Detroit for what would be his final performance. After the show he was taken to the Hospital with what doctors believed to be a ruptured appendix. Houdini died of peritonitis at the age of 52.

Houdini was buried in New York on November 4, 1926, with over two thousand in attendance. He left instructions to his wife on how to attempt to contact his spirit in the hereafter. Bess tried for ten successive years to reach him after his death, but to no avail. Seances continue to be held on Halloween by magicians worldwide to this day.

There are those who believe Houdini may have been poisoned. His attempt to debunk the work of fake spiritualists may have prompted an attempt on his life. Arsenic or some other deadly substance could possibly have caused his death. In 2007, Houdini's grandnephew tried to have Houdini's remains exhumed in order to search for evidence of poisoning. As of this writing the court has not consented to the exhumation.

HOUDINI'S SCHOOL OF MAGIC

SOME HISTORY OF MAGIC

Watching a magic show on stage or television doesn't begin to teach you about magic. The way it started, how it developed, and why you are seeing the particular tricks and effects will be explained.

Magic, in the beginning, was the mother of all the arts and sciences and captured the minds and spirits of all those who saw it. In exploring the genesis of magic, some of it' s key figures, and its most recognizable tricks, we can begin to understand its importance and the reason it is still popular today.

THE OLDEST TRICK

One of the oldest tricks in the world is the venerable Cups and Balls. Some old Egyptian papyri manuscripts mention it and the descriptions of it continued through Greece and Rome. It was so popular that it was a common subject of artists throughout history and is still as popular around the world today as it was in Egypt's early days. The apparatus consists of three cups without handles and a number of small balls. In Egypt it was probably performed with clay pots and balls of stuffed cloth, while in India they used wooden cups with little knobs on top, and Japanese magicians used their typically small teacups. To perform the trick the Egyptians and Indians squatted on the ground, the Turks knelt on carpets, and in Greece and Rome the performer worked behind a small table.

Seneca the Younger (5 BC- 65 AD), Roman philosopher and writer, wrote, "It's in the very trickery that it pleases me. But show me how the trick is done and I have lost my interest therein." His sentiment is a good reason why magicians never volunteer how to do their tricks. Years later, Alciphron of Athens (ca. 150 AD), a Greek playwright, wrote a description of what the trick looked like in his day. "A man came forward and placed on a three-legged table three small dishes, under which he concealed some little white pebbles. These he placed one by one under the dishes, and then, I do not know how, he made them appear all together under one." He also admitted that the feat "rendered me almost speechless and made me gape in surprise."

Most of the surprise came at the end of the routine, naturally, when out of the cups were produced much larger balls, or live mice (China) or baby chicks (Egypt), or strange objects like lumps of coal, oranges, or even glasses of wine.

It was such a popular trick through the thousands of years since its origin, that as well as being eye-catching, it has been a foremost subject for artists. The only other pastime in Europe that might be the subject for more drawings and paintings would be that of people playing cards.

Hieronymus Bosch (ca. 1460-1516) created the most popular painting of a magician doing the trick for a gathered crowd, while Peter Breughel (ca. 1520-1569) put it into three or four of his bizarre masterpieces. It has also been a popular way to caricature politicians who have hoodwinked the public, especially in the French newspapers of the 19th century. Great artists, like Honoré Daumier, even went to prison for these daring mockeries of the upper classes, because everyone readily recognized what their drawings of magicians hoodwinking the public really meant.

Undoubtedly the most interesting and amazing of the Cups and Balls conjurors was Mathias Buchinger (1674-1739), a German showman who was born without hands or legs but became an expert shooter, painter, musician, and bowler, as well as magician.

THE OLDEST NAME IN MAGIC

The name of the oldest magician known to the public throughout most of the world is that of Merlin, King Arthur's mentor, advisor, and wizard. We know little of his supposed date or place of birth or of his background, but he is usually believed to be from Wales, that mysterious region of southwest England. The ballads credit Merlin (or Myrddin in Welsh) with being an enchanter who knew how to control people, an advisor to Arthur and his Round Table of knights, a seer who knew what was in the future. He was the man who flew the stones of Stonehenge from Ireland to the Salisbury Plain in Britain. He was even credited with living backward in time so he knew the future but not the past. Legend has it that he was tricked into his tomb to be sealed there alive until Britain again needed his help.

He was the quintessential magician and it's a pity that we don't know if he really existed. There have been more fiction stories written about him than there have been about King Arthur, the most famous one being *Le Morte d'Arthur* by Sir Thomas Mallory in 1470. More modern versions include *The Sword in the Stone* by T.H. White and the modern Arthur/Merlin trilogy by Mary Stewart that begins with *The Crystal Cave*. Merlin has become so famous that his name alone means "magic" to anyone who hears it.

IN THE RENAISSANCE

Although the innovations and advancements made in the Renaissance era began in Italy in the fourteenth century, it wasn't until Gutenberg perfected the moveable type printing press in 1452 that knowledge, education, and creative thinking really began to blossom. The unbelievably rapid spread of books and knowledge created more readers and sparked individual thinking in those readers. There was a lively interest in all of the sciences and the everyday man began to learn that magic and witchcraft were figments of superstition and folklore.

Roger Bacon (ca. 1220-1292), a Franciscan friar, dabbled in alchemy, philosophy and science, and possibly a little conjuring. He wrote "there are men who create illusions by the rapidity of the movements of their hands, or by the assumption of various voices, or by ingenious apparatus, or by performing in the dark, or by means of confederacy".

Entertainers who specialized in conjuring tricks could now come out from under the dirty cloud of censure and prohibition fostered by ignorance and superstition. People were becoming aware of the difference between someone who claimed to be an apostle of the black arts and someone who merely liked to do card tricks. But, like all superstition, the suspicions died hard. Even Louis IX (1214-1270), although he encouraged literature, the arts, and legal reform, tried to banish all conjurors and acrobats from France. Right up until the early twentieth century people were still being accused, imprisoned, and executed for being witches.

Various manuscripts and books from the Renaissance not only give us names and brief descriptions of conjurors (who are strictly magic entertainers) of that time, but some actually describe how to do the tricks.

In about 1564 in Switzerland, Johann Wier wrote an educational book called *De praestigiis daemonum*, and tried to explain that conjurors were merely entertainers, but he didn't give any examples. It wasn't until 1584 that Reginald Scot, a British country squire and justice of the peace, who was appalled at the ease with which old women and clever entertainers could be accused of witchcraft and burned at the stake, decided to do something.

After taking some lessons from a Frenchman living in London, he wrote his famous *Discoverie of Witchcraft*, and actually exposed some of the more common feats of conjuring, as well as a couple of stage illusions used by actors. The book was not an overnight success, but it did get noticed because King James I ordered it burned by the public hangman in 1601.

After James's reign the book was republished time and again, and is now one of the jewels of any well-stocked magic antiquarian library.

The first conjuror who really gained an international reputation was Hieronymus Scotto (ca. 1545-ca. 1602). He was so good that he was responsible for King James I making the remark that "Satan taught man tricks with cards and dice." Scotto was an excellent sleight-of-hand performer, who was a roving diplomat for Holy Roman Emperor Rudolf II, and performed for court officials in Spain, Britain, Germany, Italy, France, and even Czechoslovakia. He is also the first magician to have left a picture of him, a copper engraving done in 1592 by Dominicus Custodis. Shortly after a successful performance for Queen Elizabeth and her court in 1602, he vanished. Not a bad ending for a magician.

MAGIC SHOWMEN

Now that life wasn't quite so dangerous for magicians and they didn't have to hide their skills and names, they began to become bolder than life. For the first of these we come again to Mathias Buchinger, mentioned earlier. Although born with just stumps for legs and without arms (his hands

SOME HISTORY OF MAGIC

were attached directly to his shoulders), he was a very accomplished person. He was the ninth and last child of a well-to-do family of Nürnberg (Nuremberg), and received a good education. After the death of his parents he embarked on a performing career, excelling in all that he attempted. His first shows were in 1709 and included playing musical instruments, exhibiting his marksmanship with a musket or pistol, and some conjuring including his Cups and Balls skills.

Another very famous magic performer of the time and who died a rich man, was Isaac Fawkes (1675-1731). We don't know for sure from whom he learned his magic, but he was an important exhibitor at Bartholomew Fair from 1720-1731, a headliner of those days. He performed small effects like producing eggs and a live chicken from a bag, coin tricks, and flashy card tricks.

The first of the super-promoters was a German by the name of Gustavus Katterfelto (1730-1799). He not only advertised constantly with unbounded superlatives, but also always carried a black cat with him and claimed that the feline was his "familiar," an animal that allied him with witches and warlocks. When he performed his shows that combined magic, scientific oddities, and mechanical wonders, he wore an academic robe and a square black hat. The rest of his costume consisted of the court dress of satin knee breeches, shoes with silver buckles, and his collection of medals and ribbons. He was a member of the French Royal Academy of Sciences and Belles Lettres, and evidently knew quite a bit about medicine and natural philosophy. He freely treated many victims during a London influenza epidemic.

A magician born in the American colonies entered the European theatrical scene at this point and scared most of his audiences nearly to death. He had been born as Jacob Meyer (1734-1800?), but he changed his name to Jacob Philadelphia, in honor of the city of his birth. His first command performance was for Russia's Catherine the Great in 1772 and he continued to travel and perform in Europe. Part of his theatrical shows included the production of ghostly figures by the use of a magic lantern, a simple projector of art on glass slides that could be projected onto clouds of smoke. These dark seances, complete with spooky sound effects,  raised the hair of his audiences after pulling the money out of their pockets. He lived in Germany when not touring, never returning to the United States. No one knows when or where he died.

The King of the Charlatans was a mysterious personage known as Count Cagliostro. Some say that he was born Giuseppe Balsamo in Sicily, but later scholars say they were two separate men. If so, then no one knows where Cagliostro came from, where or how he learned his tricks, or how he was able to live such a rich life. He mixed Masonic mystery with occult explanations and presented what seemed to be miracles that he said could be performed by any man who undertook training in the magic arts. He didn't have to advertise in the newspapers because word of mouth spread faster than printed news and he was free with his healing of poor people. He established a number of Freemasons' lodges in Europe, and was always surrounded by rich men wanting to be members. Cagliostro has been called "the last magician of the Middle Ages and the first spiritualist of the nineteenth century." A very interesting movie was made about this mystery man no one really knew, and its star and director, Orson Welles (also a very accomplished magician), called it *Black Magic*.

A great performer who started in an unusual way was Pinetti (1750-1800). Born Giuseppe Merci, his innkeeper father made sure he received a classical education. Giuseppe went on to become a professor of physics in Rome. His students exclaimed about his diverting method of presenting his demonstrations, as did some friends and guests, so he decided to perform for larger audiences to acquire money. Combining his scientific knowledge with the conjuring of the day, Pinetti created a very successful show that played all over Europe, including special performances for royalty. He retired with a fortune in Russia and devoted the rest of his life to ballooning.

THE NEW BREED

At this time newspapers were gaining in popularity and even small towns had a local weekly. It became very important for a performer to call on the editor as soon as he arrived in town so that stories and gossip could circulate even before he advertised his shows. Showmen no longer had to depend on just the written word to bring in audiences as they could now carry artwork of themselves in the form of metal or wood engravings to be added to their ads. Handing one of these to the local printer along with a copy of the text guaranteed that their display advertising would always appear the way they wanted it.

The first American-born magician to become a famous performer in his own country, rather than Europe, was Richard Potter (1786-

1835). He was the mulatto son of Sir Charles Frankland, tax collector for the port of Boston, and attended school through the elementary grades. Signing on as a cabin boy to a ship captain friend of his father's, he wound up in England, became an assistant to Scottish magician John Rannie (ca. 1770-1830), and eventually returned to Boston. When Rannie retired in 1814, Potter began travelling the East Coast from Quebec to Alabama. He was very successful with his show consisting of small tricks, including the now famous Cups and Balls, and sometimes feats of fire eating. Potter died in 1835 after a very successful career.

A French magician who first performed a number of tricks that are today's classics of magic, was Philippe, the stage name of Jacques Andre Noé Talon (1802-1878). He immigrated to England to become a candy maker and later learned magic in Scotland. Touring the British Isles, he improved his show every year before returning to France. There, in Paris, he built his own theatre and began an impressive career. He would open his show by stepping out onto the darkened stage, then upon the firing a pistol, hundreds of candles would instantly light. It was probably the first application of electricity to the art of conjuring, and had to be a most impressive sight. In the second half of his presentation, he featured magic he had learned from a troupe of Chinese. These tricks included the Linking Rings, performed for the first time by a non-oriental magician, and a sensational trick of producing three large bowls of water from a spangled shawl.

THE FRENCH GENIUS

Jean Eugène Robert (1805-1871), who became France's greatest magician, saw one of Philippe's shows when he was still a watchmaker and was inspired to become a conjuror. In 1845 at the age of forty, Robert-Houdin (he added his wife's surname to his own) opened his first professional engagement in a small theatre in Paris. The opening show was a disaster, due mostly to stage fright, but his second night went exactly as it should and he began to gather his confidence. Success followed success and he began to travel in order to find new and richer audiences. In spite of lacking knowledge of the English language, Britain took to him and his show became a sensation. Two of his sons helped him present some of the larger illusions, like the levitation and the production of a number of objects, including a boy, from a flat portfolio that had been shown empty to begin with.

An accomplished mechanic, he was forever investigating new scientific principles. Together, these two interests made Robert-Houdin famous in more than one field. His automata were mechanical masterpieces, the Singing Lesson in particular. This piece of brass clockwork statuary showed a gowned lady teaching a nightingale to sing. In three tries, she would whistle a short tune and the bird would then warble its attempt until finally succeeding. All the time the bird cocks his head to listen to his mistress, turns himself on the perch, ruffles his wings and tail, and his bill opens and closes in rhythm with his singing. The Brass Magician is an equal marvel as a brass Chinese magician raises two cups from a table and shows some twenty different objects under them at different times, and then vanishes the objects completely. His foray into electricity gained him a medal for creating the first alarm clock in 1844. His estate at Saint-Gervais was wired for all sorts of electrical work such as feeding the horses, notifying the house when mail had been delivered, a gate that opened by itself, and a steeple clock that never needed winding. He also invented the opthalmascope that is still used today to look into the interior of the eyeball. He was an amazing man and is still honored by the French public.

Probably the most confusing magician to magic historians took the name Signor Blitz (1810-1877). At one time there were as many as six magicians working as Signor Blitz, and four or five more since then. The one born as Antoni van Zandt, in Deal, England, is the one who became the most famous. The British Blitz advertised himself as a former assistant and pupil of Jacob Philadelphia, but this cannot be verified. He did, however, have a distinguished career in Europe, Britain, and the United States. He wasn't satisfied in just fooling his audiences he also wanted them to have fun, so it's possible to call him the first comedy magician. Through the years he also featured plate spinning and ventriloquism, and believed in giving all he had for each performance.

THE WIZARD OF THE NORTH

John Henry Anderson (1814-1874) was born near Aberdeen, Scotland, and became apprenticed to a magician known as "Big Scott" in 1831. He went on his own in 1837. In 1839 he appropriated poet Sir Walter Scott's nickname of "The Wizard of the North" and married Big Scott's daughter in 1842. He played all of the major theatres in the British Isles, toured Europe, and continued around the world appearing in Australia and doing two tours of the United States. Anderson was a master of

SOME HISTORY OF MAGIC

advertising; where other performers were content with putting up one large poster in a town; he would have posters cover almost every blank wall available. He wanted people to know his name and he carried with him a wooden butter mold that put his name on the pats given to customers of inns near the theatre where he was appearing. His shows included prizes awarded for puzzle and riddle contests. Booklets were for sale after each show (these alone went into 250 editions, if you believe Anderson!), plus others that praised his skills to all readers. Appearing before the royal family of England at least twice gave him the reason to print thousands of copies of those programs and to also strike medals with his face and the dates of the performances. All of his children, three daughters and two sons, worked with him in the show at various times and two of them went out on their own. J.H. Anderson, Jr., stayed in the United States when his father finished his second tour in the colonies and played successfully for the next eleven years in the U.S., Canada, and Britain. A daughter, Alice, also took to the boards as a magic performer, but was drowned in New Zealand in a boating accident after only eight years of performing on her own.

PROFESSOR HOFFMANN

At this point, there occurred in England an event that was to change the face of magic for all time. A book was published with the title of "Modern Magic" and its author was a Professor Hoffmann. The book was actually written by Angelo J. Lewis (1839-1919), a barrister, who wanted to protect his name from sensationalism. Its 511 pages were filled with complete descriptions of how to do all the popular tricks of the day, with excellent wood engravings to show exactly how everything worked.

The year before, in 1875, Hoffmann's magic was serialized in Routledge's Every Boy's Magazine, and the entire manuscript was published in one book. It was an immediate success and sold out the entire edition of two thousand copies in only seven weeks. By 1919, Modern Magic had sold over 26,000 copies, not including all of the pirated editions, and had been sent to magic enthusiasts all over the world. The first American edition was published by Routledge, but was printed in England. The first edition printed in America was by David McKay in 1904 and has since been printed over and over again for American readers. The name of Professor Hoffmann on a book proved to be magic in itself and he went on to produce many more titles. Hoffmann broke the dam of self-imposed censorship in the world of magic and now all the performers wanted to write books. And many of them did. Each year brought forth more and more titles, some published by giant companies, others privately printed for circulation exclusively among magicians. The year 1876 marked the end of real secrecy in the world of magic and is also considered the last year for antiquarian magic books, as all the books since then are referred to as being modern.

RABBITS IN HATS

The image of a rabbit in a top hat is recognized almost worldwide in its representation of magic and sleight-of-hand, but how did it come to be?

Back in 1726, Mary Toft ran into her home in Guildford, England, quite upset. She claimed to have been assaulted by a rabbit! Her husband, Joshua, didn't know what to make of her story but when she became ill that night he sent for the best physician in the area, Dr. John Howard. The good doctor made no statement at that time, but continued to look in on Mary as her physical condition wavered through the following months. Finally, on the night of 27 September, Dr. Howard informed the village that Mary had given birth to five little white rabbits. But that was merely the beginning, as Mary continued to drop the furry creatures every once in a while through the next few weeks.

Even in those days news traveled fast and the king, George I, quickly heard about Mary's unusual productions and sent two physicians for second opinions. They agreed with Dr. Howard, but the king wasn't satisfied, so he then sent Britain's famous skeptic, Sir Richard Manningham, FRS, and that's when Mary began to have problems.

Being a fastidious man, he wouldn't leave Mary's side for all the time he observed her. No rabbits appeared. A little later he even had the audacity to have her bundled off to a hospital in London, where she was still watched as closely, but now in shifts. Still no rabbits appeared.

Next thing the public knew, Sir Richard had had Mary arrested. At her trial he produced a deposition from a hospital porter swearing that he had procured a rabbit for Mary. Mary broke down and confessed that she'd only wanted some fun and a little attention. Well, she got it! The entire country went wild with the story of Mary Toft, the girl who gave birth to rabbits and fooled the high and mighty city doctors. Songs were composed and bawdy broadsides were printed, and somewhere, during all the laughter, a traveling magician had an idea. That night he borrowed a hat, showed it empty, and produced a rabbit. He probably didn't even have to say anything.

Mary Toft became even more famous by a very famous artist, William Hogarth, who featured her labors in one of his great engravings, entitled "Credulity, Superstition and Fanaticism." So you can thank a serving girl for the most lasting of magic's symbols - the rabbit in the hat.

GOLDEN AGE OF MAGIC

Performing magicians are presently enjoying the Second Golden Age of Magic, which started in the mid-1960s and has completed over forty years. The First Golden Age was during the heyday of vaudeville in the United States, from about 1890 until 1930, but music halls and variety theatres are still common in Europe as they didn't let their theatrical arts die out.

There were a number of contributing factors to that exciting time when vaudeville came into its own. Saloons and beer gardens with singing waiters, dancing girls, and singers were popular, and every little town had a local hall available for rent by the Masons, the Odd Fellows, or the local volunteer fire department. Dime museums with live acts were opening in most of the large cities, and the local theatres were booking acts for variety bills of their own.

Then, two men in New York were responsible for presenting variety shows that were fit for the entire family, and started creating customers that went to the theatre every week as a family outing. Tony Pastor and B.F. Keith created clean theatres, fined the performers for improper words or actions during their acts, and raised the salaries of the better performers. Pastor had a total of three theatres in his time, but only one at a time. Keith started buying theatres as fast as he could, and thus created the first vaudeville circuit; a chain of theatres that could keep an act working for a solid period of time by moving to a different theatre every week.

VAUDEVILLE CIRCUITS

In 1910 there were about 2,000 smalltime theatres across the country, and probably another 300 that handled the big time acts. By 1923 Keith's circuit handled almost 400 theatres, the Orpheum circuit controlled another 300, and there were about 200 large independent houses. Besides the two big theatrical circuits, there were about twenty circuits of small-time vaudeville. So, at this time any good act, and a number of poor ones, could work for years without working the same theatre twice. In fact, most acts did the same act almost as long as they could work, about 35 to 40 years, without changing the basic act. Little bits of business and some jokes or songs would be changed, but not the basic routine.

In the cities the audiences kept growing, and theatres were built to accommodate the larger crowds. From 1891 to 1910 there were over twelve million immigrants, most of them locating in the cities, so that when coupled with the natural increase in the birth rate, the population from 1900 to 1910 soared by over sixteen million people, to over ninety-two million for our growing country. Considering that the average theatre probably seated between two and five hundred customers, and that the average act worked two to three shows a day, you can understand how David Copperfield works for more people in one television special than any vaudeville act in their entire lifetime.

Vaudeville was made up, basically, of higher paid specialists. Its acts came from the dime museums and beer gardens, and had proved themselves as people who were entertainers and audience-pleasers. Around the turn of the century the least of the acts were getting sixty to a hundred dollars a week, with many stars getting a thousand a week, and a few rarities getting as much as $2,500 each and every week. Right off the top of that salary, the agent handling the act got his ten percent, and sometimes the theatre circuit took an additional five percent for being nice enough to hire the act. Out of the remainder the act had to pay all of its own expenses, the biggest of which was transportation. Only the Orpheum, the circuit covering the western states, paid for train travel due to the longer distances covered than in the eastern states. Most big cities had theatrical boarding houses that not only included meals as part of the price, but the price was slightly lower than a hotel. When working the smaller cities and towns, the act had to pay hotel rates, and they never got the discounted commercial rate available to salesmen because of the prejudice against show

SOME HISTORY OF MAGIC

folk. Working, packing, unpacking, and working again and again, also created wear and tear on wardrobe, props, and scenery, if they carried their own. All of the repairs, upkeep, and replacement of these items were also out of pocket expenses for the act, and could be quite costly for custom-made equipment. Animal acts had the additional expense of food for their charges, and in the case of seals and cats, their requirements may not be available in that week's town.

SMALL-TIME ACTS

There were all kinds of acts in vaudeville, including some people who weren't actors but had done something newsworthy. Champion prizefighters, tree choppers, and elocution contest winners shared programs with the dog acts, jugglers, singers, and hoofers. Even people who had been acquitted of murder, or were about to go to trial, were sometimes booked at the local theatre to tell their story and be ogled by the ticket holders. There were single acts where only one person traveled from town to town to work, or as many as ten people in a repertory company that presented small plays or musical presentations.

Magic acts were also sold in a variety of numbers and styles. The smaller acts would have up to three people, and an illusionist who presented the larger tricks could carry as many as six or eight assistants. Many of the single acts would appear in front of the house curtain ("in one", in stage parlance) to give the stagehands time to set up the next act that had a lot of scenery or a large number of props. Magicians who worked "in one" were usually card manipulators, or comedy acts that depended on just a few props and a lot of funny remarks. Many of these wizards were good enough that today's magicians still honor their names and skills. Jack Merlin, Si Stebbins, Nate Leipzig, and Paul Valadon depended mostly on card tricks. Gus Fowler vanished, produced, and changed watches and clocks. Frank Van Hoven started with a serious act, but after developing a routine with two kid volunteers and a block of ice he became one of the funniest acts in the theatre. There were probably an additional 200 or more magicians who have been mostly forgotten by now.

There were many oriental acts working vaudeville, with the Chinese coming to Europe and America long before the Japanese because Japan denied emigration to its citizens until the late 1860s. The greatest of the Chinese troupes were headed by Ching Ling Foo and Han

Ping-Chien, with individual performers like Long Tack Sam and Kuma. Famous Japanese acts worked under the leadership of Ten Ichi and as the Asahi Troupe, and with a few singles like Tenkai. Oriental magicians became such a bookable novelty that many occidental magicians put on yellow grease paint, silk robes, and worked under fictitious oriental names. The most successful of these was William Ellsworth Robinson (1861-1918), a Scottish American who was a very clever magician, inventor and performer, as well as an excellent actor. Ching Ling Foo, during his first American tour, published a thousand-dollar challenge to other magicians for a magic contest, claiming naturally, that he would emerge as the better magician. Robinson adopted a Chinese disguise, devised some oriental-looking tricks, and showed up to do magic battle. After seeing Robinson perform, Ching immediately backpedaled and claimed that the challenge was for American magicians only and not the better Chinese ones. The event garnered a lot of newspaper publicity for Robinson, especially after he showed the newsmen that he really was an American. In later years he went on to become world famous as Chung Ling Soo, and even after his death many people still thought he was oriental.

VAUDEVILLE STARS

Some illusionists worked only vaudeville as a large act, but limited to thirty or forty minutes for their turn. The Great Leon (1876-1951) not only worked with four or five assistants, but was good enough that he could change his show every other year or so. Probably his most famous illusion was "Fire and Water", where a girl vanished from a blazing paper cone and reappeared inside a glass tank of water.

Horace Goldin (1873-1939) was known as The Whirlwind Illusionist, and he claimed that he worked so fast that if you turned to speak to the person next to you that you'd miss a trick. He was born in Poland and didn't immigrate to America until his teens. He also fell into a well when he was very young. The combination of these two circumstances meant that he spoke English with a very strong accent and with a stammer because of his fall.

As a young man he had learned the Egg Bag from Albini, and started playing dime museums with his small repertoire. After a year or so of playing as many as twenty-five shows a day for ten dollars a week, he became very confident and smooth. He then played six shows at Tony Pastor's theatre to show his skills to larger and better audiences, but because of his selection of corny jokes coupled with his speech problems, the newspaper reviewer suggested that future audiences "stuff their ears with cotton." Because of this review Goldin immediately started working as a silent act. Fortunately this decision let him work at breakneck speed to do twice as much magic as the next magician.

As an established headliner in show business in later years, he tried a number of innovative ideas in his magic. For one, he was the first magician to change a girl into a roaring live lion. He was also the first magician to transfer a person from the stage onto the screen of a motion picture. He was also the magician who did the Sawing a Woman in Half for more audiences than any other, either in America or in Europe, even though the inventor of the original trick was an Englishman. Goldin, however, cut his girl in half with a buzzsaw rather than a simple crosscut saw. Another of his startling effects was when he walked up to one of his male assistants, punched a hole through the man's body and then proceeded to pass objects, liquids, and his hand through the hole.

AMERICA'S ILLUSIONISTS

There were two other very famous American magicians who became household names, and with very similar lifetimes. Both Thurston and Blackstone started in small theatres and vaudeville, and then became the leading illusionists of America.

Howard Thurston (1869-1936) was on his way to become a theological student when he witnessed a show by Herrmann the Great. He skipped school, learned magic, and started travelling and playing small theatres with small magic, primarily card tricks. In 1898 both he and his idol, Herrmann, were playing theatres in Denver. He had recently invented a version of the Rising Cards, where cards selected by members of the audience were caused to rise into the air from the deck. Between shows he demonstrated the trick for Herrmann, who admitted he was fooled, and Thurston immediately jumped on the chance for publicity. The next day the *Denver Post* reported that Howard Thurston was "the man who fooled Herrmann".

That article didn't make Thurston famous, however, and he still had to struggle through smalltime show business. He slowly worked his way up the ladder until he was playing the better vaudeville houses,

HOUDINI'S SCHOOL OF MAGIC

and then traveled with Harry Kellar for a year as a feature performer in that show. Then, on May 16, 1908, at the Ford Theatre in Washington, D.C., Kellar publicly turned his show over to Thurston as his magic successor. Over the next twenty years Thurston made the show into the leading magic show in America. He would have retired with a fortune, but he kept putting his money into the wrong investment schemes like Florida land for orange groves and the wrong inventions like an anti-snoring device. He collapsed from a paralytic stroke after a show in Charleston, West Virginia, and died a few months later.

Harry Blackstone (1885-1965) was the perfect example of having to adapt to a changing show business. He and his brother, Pete, did a comedic magic act in vaudeville, and gradually built larger and larger shows. When the illusionist Albini died in Chicago, Blackstone bought several of the illusions, and now considered himself an illusionist. Still being short of money, however, he bought some posters that a printer was holding because another magician never paid the bill. So, for a year or so, at least until the posters ran out, Blackstone worked as Fredrik the Great.

He started gaining a reputation as a performer who had a wonderful rapport with his audiences. With his bushy hair, the attitude of "let's have fun," and a voice made for use in theatres, he captivated audiences all over the United States. His magic was fascinating as he vanished a horse, produced a camel (but only for a few shows as the camel had ideas of his own). He produced and vanished a flock of ducks, as well as putting his female assistants through all sorts of torture that turned out to be harmless. He even toured his version of the famous Hindu Rope Trick, where a rope is levitated into the air, a boy climbs it, and then the boy vanishes and the rope falls to the stage in a puff of smoke.

When movies made vaudeville vanish, he shortened the show and played it between pictures in movie houses. He then built a full-evening show (about an hour and a half of all magic) and toured it through America's legitimate theatres and auditoriums. During World War II he played hundreds of shows for the United Service Organizations in army, navy, and air corps bases, and then went back to touring his magic and appearing on television. He retired in 1959 and moved to Hollywood where he lived only a block away from the Magic Castle, a private club where magicians entertain themselves and guests.

WORLD TRAVELLERS

There were also a number of magicians who became famous magicians in other countries before they became headliners in the United States. Alexander Herrmann (1844-1896) grew up in France in a family full of magicians. He toured as a young man with his older brother, Carl, through Europe and played all of the capital cities. They worked in America three times before Alexander went his own way in 1874, with an agreement that Alexander would play only in North and South America and Carl would have Europe.

Working as Herrmann the Great, he and his wife, Adelaide, built a beautiful and mystifying show that played the best theatres for the next twenty years. He was a consummate magician, performing tricks all during the day as well as in his evening performances. He would mystify and delight shopkeepers, people on the street and especially waiters in restaurants. Objects would be produced from the most unusual places, utensils would vanish, and money would do all sorts of strange things while in his presence.

Onstage his illusions brought him overwhelming publicity, as they were not only startling in effect, but also dressed in splendor and good taste. One of his most famous, and most dangerous, was doing the Bullet Catch. He had a squad of five riflemen who fired bullets at him, and he caught all of them on a china plate held in front of him. Fortunately, in the years that he did the trick, he never had an accident.

He not only purchased a great estate on Long Island in New York, a yacht, and a private railroad car, but he also had his own theatre for a while in New York. He averaged $100,000 a year in his last years, and this was without any income taxes and at a time when the average working man was getting $250 a year.

After he died in his railroad car between shows, his wife, Adelaide, brought in his nephew, Leon, to replace him. The act was then known as Herrmann the Great, but it played for only three years. Adelaide and Leon split company, sued each other over the use of the name of Herrmann the Great, and Adelaide went out on her own. She became a very successful headliner until she retired in 1928 just before the end of vaudeville. She brought a fitting close to the great Herrmann name.

The Great Lafayette (1872-1911) gave a thrilling show that combined magic with quick-change transformations. He would open the show as an artist, do a couple of illusions to produce girls, and then immediately change into a Chinese magician to produce animals and bowls of water. He then became an imitation John Philip Sousa (the famous composer and bandleader) to lead the band and do a few music-theme magic effects. He not only carried all of his own scenery and a number of assistants, but also his pet dog, a lion, and a horse. He and two assistants died in a theatre fire in Edinburgh, Scotland.

William Robinson, before he put on the disguise of a Chinese magician, was in demand as a mechanic and inventor for other magicians. One of his first successes was when he used the principle of Black Art that had been developed by Max Auzinger in Germany. This is an act that is done on a stage draped in black velvet using props that are painted all white or light yellow. Using the principle that you can't see black objects when they're against a black background, the magician (dressed in white) works with one or more assistants invisibly dressed in black to accomplish some amazing illusions. Later he became a valued mechanic for Kellar and Herrmann. While with Kellar he invented and built two very successful illusions, one of which produced a girl from a giant oyster shell. Later, when working with Herrmann, he would sometimes perform an entire show as Herrmann by using makeup and adopting the stage manner of the magician, who wanted a night off from his busy schedule.

After he left the Herrmann troupe he wrote a book for magicians while running a magic shop in New York. The following year, 1900, he was asked by an agent to do an oriental act and he began the best part of his life. As Chung Ling Soo, he eventually carried an immense show with as many as ten assistants and mechanics, with loads of scenery. He established his own workshop in England with highly skilled wood and metal workers. Robinson would take over a theatre for an entire week, not only as the complete program but also with changes of the show during the week. He was truly one of the most remarkable of illusionists. He died as the result of a mechanical failure in his feature trick, "Catching a Bullet".

Harry Kellar (1849-1922) was a true success story in the world of magic. He was raised in Erie, Pennsylvania, but ran away from home and was living in Canandaigue, New York, when he saw a performance of magic by The Fakir of Ava, whose offstage name was Isaiah H. Hughes (1813-1891). A month or so later he saw a newspaper ad in which The Fakir needed a boy assistant. He immediately made his way to Buffalo to apply for the job. The Fakir's little dog took an immediate liking to Kellar and the Fakir hired him on that recommendation. Five years later he left the act and started out to work as a magician himself. Years of hard work, many disappointments, and

SOME HISTORY OF MAGIC

near starvation finally lead him to a job with the Davenport Brothers. Ira (1839-1911) and William (1841-1877) Davenport had put together an act that espoused spiritualism by being tied inside a cabinet and then having musical instruments play as various objects are tossed around. Kellar toured with them for five years, working his way up to be their manager and booking agent, before he again went out on his own. This time, however, he began having great success in the Caribbean, Central and South America, before touring the world.

In 1884 he brought his full-evening show before an American audience in New York, and he was on his way to total success as America's leading magician. The cabinet trick, that he had learned from the Davenports and had even improved over the years, was in every show he did and probably garnered more publicity than did any of his other tricks, until he introduced The Dream of Princess Karnac. In this illusion he caused a woman to levitate from a couch up about ten feet into the air without any covering and in bright stage lighting. It was a beautiful mystery, and even after he retired in 1908 he continued to improve it, and it is still a first-class miracle today.

Kellar and Houdini, in spite of being two very different personalities and showmen, became very close friends. Kellar, ever the dignified gentleman, and Houdini, the rumpled and belligerent escape artist, had the highest respect for each other. In two or three collections today there are most of the letters they wrote to each other about other magicians, fatherly advice from Kellar to Houdini about tricks and business, and the latest magic news and gossip from Houdini to Kellar. In 1907 Houdini gave a gigantic party for Kellar with about 200 magicians to give an appreciation for Kellar's superb talent, and to vote him as the first Dean of American Magicians. Then, again in 1917, Houdini arranged a special show, apparently to benefit the Red Cross, with the leading magicians of the time as the performers, and with Kellar to do an act at the end. Instead, it had been arranged as a secret tribute to Kellar. It was highly successful and generated a glowing thank-you letter from Kellar to Houdini.

Harry Alvin Jansen (1883-1955) was another worldfamous illusionist, who performed under the name of Dante. He was born in Denmark, and came to the U.S. at the age of six. He learned magic as a schoolboy hobby, and started doing shows for local organizations in his teens. By the time he was 19 he had an hour show and was playing theatres farther and farther from home. After marrying a musician and having his first son, he decided to create some roots so he opened a magic company in Chicago and played only local engagements. In 1911, Jansen got an offer he couldn't refuse. He left to play Australia and the Far East, and he and his growing family didn't return for four years. American dates were played for a few years, and in 1922 he again went on a foreign tour. As Dante, he continued to play countries around the world until Berlin in August of 1939. Dante heard that Hitler was going to invade Poland, that meant total war in Europe because of all the alliances in force, and he had six hours to get his company out of Germany and to a neutral country. They made a mad dash to Sweden and just made it before the gates of Germany closed on everyone still inside.

The troupe disbanded and Dante, his family of five, and Moi-Yo Miller, his principal female assistant, got visas to the United States. Through the years of World War II he played all over North America, and then made another foreign tour to England after the war. Returning to America he retired in California and spent his remaining six years appearing in small parts in movies and on television.

THE MOVIES

Moving pictures, which hit the public in 1904, and radio, that debuted in 1920, quickly cut into the theatre-going public. In 1907, three years after the first successful showing of a motion picture, over 2,000,000 people a day were sitting in nickelodeon theatres watching the flickering images on white sheets. It didn't take a theatre, only an empty store with a sheet at one end and rows of chairs to fill up the rest of the space, and an entrepreneur had a motion picture show. Radio didn't even need that much room, just enough space for an engineer, some cabinets of wires and tubes, and a microphone for an announcer.

But, these two inventions together soon spelled the end of vaudeville, the greatest presentation of live show business that the world had ever seen. It will probably never again be that popular, and it gave us some wonderful acts and people to savor through the stories of their successes and fading photos. Fortunately, for the world of magic, we still have some of their props and, in some cases, film of some of the great names actually showing us their skills and styles. They discovered the psychology of audiences, established the basic rules for entertaining people, and invented the principles we still use today. We owe an overwhelming debt of gratitude to those magic pioneers, and we can uphold our end by continuing to read about them, to study their methods, and to continue to build better magic based on their knowledge and talents.

WORLD WAR II

The years from 1940 to 1945 made a radical difference in show business, especially for magicians. The ten years or so that lead up to this point had been very difficult ones for performers as the old, large show theatres were converting to movies, or being torn down to make way for office buildings. Some magicians were able to make the change from stage work to presenting much smaller magic shows in nightclubs and for special events, but generally there wasn't much need for live performers.

World War II changed all of that. With the great increase in jobs to produce all of the equipment and supplies that were necessary to fight a war there were gigantic payrolls of money across the country. Floods of people moved from farms and small towns to the large cities in order to fill the jobs that needed them, and these people needed entertainment as well as houses and everyday necessities. More and more nightclubs opened and they required entertainers. Theatres began adding live performers to each evening's movies in order to gain a larger share of the excess money that was being spent. In addition, there were the tours to sell war bonds that needed entertainers to gather a crowd, and there were the troupes of United Service Organization (USO) entertainers who traveled to the various camps and naval bases to entertain the hordes of servicemen being processed and trained. Some headliners like Blackstone and Dante, cut their shows down to just three or four assistants, but still presented a full show in the camps and theatres.

A magician was a very valuable asset to the people who had to arrange these types of entertainment. Magicians didn't always need a group of musicians to back them up, they could work alone and with volunteers from the audience. They could talk to large groups of people, and they knew how to get laughs. It wasn't just the experienced vaudevillians who did these shows. Many neophyte magicians were drafted or volunteered for the armed services as patriotic Americans, but were discovered by the upper echelons to be able to entertain. They were transferred into Special Services units that created shows made up of talented GIs, and then traveled the nation and to foreign bases to provide wonder, laughs, and music.

Many of the better known professional performers from show business were GI conjurors. They were magicians like Jay Palmer, Jack Gwynne, Jay Marshall, Carl Rosini, Frank Martineau, and

Milbourne Christopher. Each of them did more than his share during the war, and each of them continued in the field of magic after they were discharged. The lesser known magicians, some of them just amateurs, always had a deck of cards or a length of rope in their personal belongings, and were delighted to do tricks for their buddies, or anyone else who happened to be in the crowd.

POSTWAR

After the war, the theatres and nightclubs that had opened to entertain the defense workers were still in business, and it didn't look like business was going to slow down. The magicians who had learned to work in clubs before the war had a distinct advantage over the others, and they quickly became well-paid headliners.

Jack Gwynne, as his family grew, put each of his sons and daughters and then grandkids into the act, and played not only large nightclubs but also the theatres that had revived vaudeville. He was a very innovative magician and created many excellent tricks that made him different from other magicians. He created a Floating Lady that he could do on a club floor, practically surrounded, as well as an unbelievable production of a stack of six fishbowls filled with water and fish.

Most of the club magicians did much smaller magic, and some strictly manipulative acts with almost no equipment. That is, they worked sleight of hand with billiard balls, cigarettes, silk handkerchiefs, and playing cards, and augmented those routines with the time tested classics of magic like the Cups and Balls, the Linking Rings, and the Dollar Bill in Cigarette.

Paul Rosini, for example, did almost all take-a-card tricks, with the Egg Bag as an opening trick and the Thumb Tie as his closer. Milbourne Christopher did an involved routine with one or two lengths of rope and two or three equally small tricks. Dai Vernon performed for a long time in the Rainbow Lounge in New York with small hand tricks, but dressed in a harlequin costume, using elegant gestures and grace, and producing a live monkey as part of the act.

Many other magicians made their living as banquet performers. Committees or companies would hire these magicians to entertain a large group of people who had just finished a banquet and wanted to relax. It wasn't as precarious a living as it sounds, and most of them

SOME HISTORY OF MAGIC

traveled all over the country and many times had to turn down jobs because their calendar was fully booked.

The big shows were on the road again as well. Blackstone and Virgil were touring the country playing all kinds of theatres, and Dante resumed the world tours that he'd done in his earlier life. Even Virgil, after building up his show in the U.S., made a five-year trip around the world taking American magic to such far-flung places as Singapore, Australia, and even India. Other large shows played the county and state fairs, becoming star attractions on the midway that also presented freak shows and exhibits of gangster cars or midget horses.

TELEVISION

Radio was progressing from just a sound box to an appliance that provided pictures as well as sound. Magic is a very visual part of show business, and magicians began working television even before it became public. A British magician by the name of Fred Culpitt was possibly the first conjuror to appear on television as he performed in an experimental BBC show in 1936. Later, American magician Milbourne Christopher was a guest on television in England in 1937, and Jay Marshall did a test on American TV in 1941. Quickly, as the need for new and different acts began to be felt by the producers, more and more magicians learned how to work in front of the hot lights and non-blinking camera.

Soon, some magicians even had their own show. One of the first was "The Magic Lady" in Hollywood in the late 1940s, which featured Gerrie Larsen, wife of magician Bill Larsen, Sr., and a good magician in her own right. She dressed in ball gowns, was assisted by a midget costumed as an elf, and presented fairytale type of magic. It was only a local station, but it was a sustaining program that ran for a couple of years. Hollywood also produced the first, and very good, network show that was called "It's Magic". It used Paul Tripp, a non-magician, who introduced and worked with a different magic act each week, with the act having the advantage of being assisted by the show's two beautiful female assistants. Soon there were magic TV shows all over the country, most of them local efforts and for local audiences, but many made the big time. Those efforts have produced the experience and appreciation for magic that has created the present magic spectaculars of the last twenty years.

HOUDINI'S SCHOOL OF MAGIC
MECCA OF MAGIC

At one time London was the center for magic in the western world. That was where Professor Hoffmann (actually a lawyer by the name of Angelo J. Lewis) wrote his wonderful books to teach newcomers how to do magic. There were, and still are, more theatres in London than any other city in the world, and all European magicians considered it an honor to perform at least one season in Britain's capital city.

Then, in the golden age of vaudeville that ran from about 1880 to 1930, New York was the new center of magic. The great magic shops that sold to magicians all over the world were here: Martinka's Magic, Hornmann Magic Company, Carl Hartz, Holden's Magic, Kanter's Magic Shop, Al Flosso, Tannen's, Abbott's, and a score of lesser stores operated here through the years. Many magicians made it their home and headquarters as they traveled about the world, and most of vaudeville was booked from that city for the circuits all over the U.S. and Europe. Resident magicians, many of them amateurs, began creating magic effects that were printed and built and sent to associates throughout the world, and these same magicians began to form clubs and associations. These local clubs soon grew, and the Society of American Magicians (founded in 1902) has grown until it has over a hundred branches across the country.

Even after vaudeville faded from the scene, New York remained the center of magicians' attention because of its many nightclubs and society events. New York was famous for its magicians, not only the stand-up performers, but for the marvelous entertainers who worked close-up magic at tables. Men like Dai Vernon, Jerry Ross, Dr. Jaks, and Mohammed Bey entertained vacationing workers visiting New York as well as the highest members of society out for an evening of fun. Then, slowly, the emphasis began shifting to Chicago. Now New York and Chicago seem to have the same types of attractions. Both need talent to entertain out-of-towners, they are both urban centers that are surrounded by resort areas that need seasonal entertainment, and they both have a large contingent of tourists and convention attendees that fill the entertainment centers after business hours.

So, why Chicago?

There isn't any one answer, but in any case, Chicago became the spot where magicians went to establish their residences and places of business. Magic dealers like Laurie Ireland, the National Magic Company, Joe Berg's Princess Magic Shop, Sam Berland, and others, drew

SOME HISTORY OF MAGIC

more and more magic money to Chicago. Some magicians became expert bartenders and made the magic bartender a staple for Chicago's annual crowds of conventions. Great magicians like Matt Schulein, Johnny Paul, Heba Haba Al, Frank Everhart, Johnny Platt, and "Senator" Clarke Crandall, became famous for fooling people right under their nose. Chicago remained the Mecca of magic through the forties and fifties, until one of the sons of a magician in Los Angeles had an idea.

In 1960, Milt Larsen, one of the two sons of Bill Larsen, Sr., was looking out of his office window in Hollywood at a Victorian mansion on the side of a hill only about quarter of a mile from him. He started visualizing a nightclub that would present only magic in all of its forms and fancies, and the idea grew and grew. He met the owner of the mansion, arranged for a very reasonable lease on the strength of a handshake, and on 2 January, 1963, he opened the Magic Castle, or the Academy of Magical Arts & Sciences as it's known on the corporation papers. It was a gigantic expansion of an idea fostered by his father, and Milt brought his brother Bill into the concept to keep it on a business basis.

It was evidently the right idea at the right time and at the right place as the Magic Castle took off like a shot. In the years that followed other cities tried to duplicate the idea, but they all failed for one reason or another. The Castle has been the background for a number of television specials and interviews, and was also the locale for one long-running series starring Bill Bixby as "The Magician". As a continuation of Larsen, Senior's, idea, they bestow a number of special fellowships and magician-of-the-year awards each year at a sold-out banquet in Hollywood.

The Magic Castle has four different show areas, and a guest (you have to be invited by a member) can possibly see six or seven different shows in an evening if they skip dinner and are quick on their feet. Each showroom presents one or more magicians for a weeklong engagement, and they have shown off almost every talented magician in the world. Some performers have not only traveled to Hollywood at their own expense, just to say that they have worked at the Magic Castle, but a large number of them have moved to Los Angeles as permanent residents.

Over the next twenty years Hollywood became the worldwide attraction for magicians and the principal provider of new magic tricks and illusions. The local magicians put on a number of magic conventions that attracted conjurors and magic historians from around the world, and also had a number of magic builders who created and assembled impossible feats for movies, television, and magic shows.

Then, again, the focus began to swing away to another city, this time to a city in the middle of nowhere. Magic had become such an attractive type of entertainment, that the producers of the shows in Las Vegas began booking more and more magicians. There had always been one or two magicians performing in Las Vegas, usually one downtown and one out on the fabulous Strip. But now hotels began competing with each other to give the public bigger and better magic acts. Magicians evolved from being a supporting act to the heady experience of headlining one of the extravaganzas that Las Vegas is famous for. Siegfried & Roy, the magicians from Germany who used a panther in their act, became the Number One Las Vegas Act year after year. Now they and their lions and tigers not only headline the show, they perform in a spectacular production especially designed for them and in their own theatre. Many small acts started working in this Mecca of American entertainment, and soon moved there as well since they were now working Las Vegas year round. The clever mechanics that build magic apparatus also came to town to be closer to their clients, and a magazine for magicians was started. Today there have been a dozen complete magic shows, including Caesars Magical World that is an authorized version of the Magic Castle, and a number of other shows that feature magicians, as well as a large number of magicians who make Las Vegas their home. Some of them are still active and work all over the country, and others have had their day in the spotlight and are now retired, but like to be where they can talk shop with other magicians.

Yes, today the Mecca of Magic is Las Vegas, the home of fantastic shows and impossible magic feats. It is a must-do trip for anyone interested in magic. The magic is well done, the shows are exciting, and almost all of the magicians are happy to meet another magician (even a newcomer to the craft) after the show. But some magicians still wonder about this second Golden Age of Magic that has lasted longer than the first one; what will happen next, and where will it take place?

No history of magic would be complete without bringing the reader's attention to Houdini's Magic Shops, located in many of the major hotels in Las Vegas.

Houdini's Magic Shops have thousands of magic trick gags, novelties, juggling supplies and magic-related books and videos. At the front of the store, live magicians perform throughout the day and evening and all purchased magic tricks are personally taught to the customer in a secret room in the back of the shop.

SOME HISTORY OF MAGIC

Houdini's is a fun place for any age. The hologram, museum, and stores offer places to see magic and magic history, not only from the past, but also in the making. Please visit us at www.houdini.com.

HOUDINI'S SCHOOL OF MAGIC

WHEN YOU DO MAGIC

Magic is the art of conjuring, a branch of entertainment that was developed over the ages by travelling actors, mountebanks, and jugglers who wanted to amuse the people around them. Through those centuries, certain performing rules and psychological principles were perfected, and that's the subject we're about to explore.

People enjoy magic. They want to be fooled and that is the strength of your magic. You will always have an eager audience. The psychological reasons why people want you to fool them, to show them something they can't explain, is a subject that can be discussed, theorized, analyzed, and debated for days, but not here. Our object is to teach you how to provide the entertainment that people want.

Basically, tricks are puzzles, little boxes with false bottoms, metal tubes with secret machining, playing cards that are printed differently than usual and puzzles that can be done by anyone who knows the secret.

Magic, on the other hand, is done by a pleasing personality that everyone believes, and involves normal happenings impossible to explain.

People are interested in other people and good magic is actually a display of personality. It's the presentation of a trick that changes that trick into magic.

Every thing you say and do is believable and interesting, you will then be an entertainer. Don't just learn the mechanics of doing tricks, make the tricks part of you by putting your personality into them. In other words, don't try to be someone else when you perform for people. Unless you become a professional magician, you'll always be doing tricks for people who know you and if you try to be someone else during those tricks, they'll be aware of it. The tricks will suffer from lack of a good presentation and you'll suffer from a display of false character. Just be you.

PREPARATION

Many tricks seem to be impromptu, that is, they appear to be done on the spur of the moment, when actually they required preparation. Don't be apprehensive when you hear the word "preparation" when being told the secret of a certain trick. A very old phrase in magic is that if the trick fools the spectator, then the method is worth it. As you learn more magic and start to analyze the reactions to your magic, you will find that the saying is true most of the time. Your repertoire should include both tricks that are impromptu and ones that need some kind of preparation. Most times the preparation is very simple and can be done long before you actually do the trick; like setting a few cards in certain spots in the deck, or doing something special to a dollar bill in your wallet. The best way to handle that type of preparation is to pretend that you never did it and that the props you're using are all completely innocent. If you believe that what you're doing is real, then your audience will believe it too.

An important part of preparation is mastering a trick, regardless of how simple it is. This means learning it, practicing the moves, rehearsing the routine, and getting ready to do it for someone else.

When you first read or are taught a trick, the first decision to make is whether the trick fits you. Will it fit your personality and will it fit your skills? Like every other craft, magic has to be learned step-by-step. You have to master the easy basics before you can tackle the more difficult skills and routines. So, look at the moves involved to see if you can do them. If you like the trick and think you can do it, then start learning it.

Each trick in this book is divided into parts and even though all parts are not used for each trick, the parts are as follows: (1) Effect, (2) Props Needed, (3) Secret, (4) Preparation, (5) Routine and (6) Important Points. The Effect is a description of exactly how the audience sees the trick. Props Needed is a list of all the objects you need to do the trick. Preparation will tell you how to get ready for the trick and any special things that might have to be done to any of your props. The Routine is every move you do in the trick, both the

WHEN YOU DO MAGIC

obvious and the secret, so the trick will work. It has to be read very carefully because one word (like faceup or facedown) can make a big difference in the trick and reading it wrong will make the trick fail miserably. The Important Points listed at the end will stress the most important moves and will sometimes give you some psychological information as well. It gives you a hint here and there so your tricks will be smoother and gain you the reputation of being a real entertainer, not just someone who is able to do a trick or two. They will also help you understand how and why magic works and how to get the best effect from the simplest trick.

PRACTICE

Go through the instructions with the objects in hand, do each move as described, and even though you have difficulty at this point, go all the way through to the end. Do it again and again so you learn the entire routine at the same time you learn the new moves. Always practice the entire routine together, not in small parts. The individual moves may need to be practiced over and over to make them easier to accomplish, but always do the whole routine. Practice the routine two or three times, then take a break to just think about what you're doing. Are there any rough spots? Can something be made simpler? Where are you having trouble?

After you've thought about the trick, go back and practice it two or three more times before you take another break. You learn better and faster if you don't make your practice sessions too long. It will also keep you from developing bad habits, that is, incorrect moves, secret moves that can be seen, unnecessary moves, and other wrong actions that you'll have to correct later. Take your time and correct them now.

At the same time, make sure that all the moves you're doing in the trick are done in a natural way. First, do the move the way it would actually be done so you can see exactly how your fingers are held and the attitude of your hands. For example, if you're learning how to vanish a coin in your hands, put the coin in your hand the way you normally would. Now do it the magic way and see if there are any differences. Either practice the magic move so there aren't any differences, or you'll have to change your normal moves to match the magic ones.

Once the moves are mastered, you should go through the routine to see how and where you can make it become more of a part of you. Can it also be simplified? Can it be associated with some place you've been or with something you've done to make it more natural? Does it involve objects that you're familiar with?

Now we're going to talk about something that is very important. There's an old saying that everyone has heard, "The hand is quicker than the eye," and you'll hear it quite often when you do your tricks. The saying, however, is mostly wrong. You might be able to move the hand fast enough to fool the eye, but the true way to fool people is to fool the brain. When you move too fast, the eye sees a blur and the brain thinks, "What happened there?" So, to get the most out of your magic and to make sure that your secret moves fool the brains of your audiences, you move in a slow, graceful, and misleading manner. All of your movements should be done in a natural motion and should be presented as though you want to make sure that no one thinks you're cheating. You are cheating, of course, and they know it, but they shouldn't even suspect when a cheating move may be taking place. We repeat, as you do the trick you have to believe that you're really doing what you pretend to be doing. The feeling of belief will transmit itself to your audience and they will also believe.

When you get to the point that you're doing the routine in a way that you feel is right, then do it three or four times in a row and time how it long it takes, right from the beginning to the last move. As you learn magic it pays to keep a list of the tricks you can do and exactly how long each one takes to perform. This will come in very handy when you start making lists of your tricks as routines. You can have a couple of routines that involve only two or three short tricks, a routine that uses tricks that have the same theme, and a couple of routines that can be done standing up in front of a crowd at a party. Once you make up those lists of routines and learn them, then you're ready to perform in public because you'll be making good magic in a smooth, professional manner.

BASIC RULES

Here are the basic rules that every magician should obey in order to become more professional.

1. Don't reveal the secret of a trick, even to your best friend. To

do so violates the first rule of magic's ethics, as you aren't the only person performing that trick. Furthermore, your friends won't think you're very clever if they find out how easily the tricks are done.

2. Don't do any trick until you have practiced it and can perform it flawlessly. Even simple tricks can be ruined if poorly performed. If a trick goes wrong, which can happen for a number of reasons other than your skill, just laugh off the result. Tell your audience that it should have been a miracle, and start right in on another trick. This is another good reason for having a set routine of tricks to follow.

3. Don't perform the same trick twice before the same audience. Even the best trick loses its mysterious effect if repeated and the secret might be revealed in the second showing. A few of magic's tricks are designed to be repeated and when you learn a new trick, you'll be told if it is one of them.

4. Don't do too many tricks at one time. Three tricks usually take the right length of time to perform and you won't bore your audience. The old show business motto is "Always leave them wanting more."

5. Don't forget to watch your newspapers and television for announcements of shows by other magicians. The best way to learn showmanship is to witness shows by experienced entertainers who have spent years perfecting their art.

All tricks should be presented in as direct and simple a manner as possible. The average person desires and enjoys being entertained by magic. Complicate the process and your tricks become problems...the entertainment gets lost.
Mohammed Bey (S. Leo Horowitz) New York, 1949

S. Leo Horowitz (1894-1971) was a noted magician in the New York area in the 1930s and 1940s, working for cafe society and at most of the better parties. He had a gracious style and an intriguing personality, but as he said above, he depended on the simplicity of his magic to make most of the impression of his performances. Other magicians have echoed the same thought for a hundred years.

To get the most out of a trick, simplify the method as well as the effect; it should be as easy as possible for you to perform it and it has to be easy for your audience to follow. The rule of thumb is that if you've come up with three methods for making a trick work (an electric motor, a clockwork mechanism, or a thread), you use the simplest, a thread. There won't be any batteries to replace or go dead when you least expect them to, you don't have to wind anything or take a chance on someone hearing the mechanics, and you can control both the speed and tension.

It doesn't apply just to the mechanics of magic, either, as the principle is just as easily applied to manipulations. If you do a card trick that has three sleights or secret moves in it, try to figure out how to eliminate one of the moves. Then, if you still like the trick, see if you can eliminate one more move to make it even more perfect. Remember that the more sleights you have in a trick, the more times there are for someone in your audience to catch you. They may only catch you in one of the three sleights that you have to do, but they only need one in order to destroy the mystery of the effect. Keep your movements as natural as possible and your sleights to a minimum.

Now many beginners interpret this to mean that all of their magic should be done with mechanical means. Not at all, it's almost just the opposite. Your two hands, when properly trained and in perfect synchronization with your mind, can duplicate any mechanical means of doing a magic trick.

Señor Mardo said, repeatedly, that his hands could duplicate any trick deck on the market, and he was right. What you have to do is strive to reach that same level of skill and knowledge.

MOVEMENT

You should, in the beginning in any case, spend as much time as possible analyzing and practicing how to do basic movements with the least amount of effort and the largest amounts of entertainment and psychology. The master of any craft or art doesn't use any unnecessary actions, and the ones used are direct, and usually in a flowing manner. Watch a classical musician as he plays his instrument; see how an artist approaches a blank surface as he begins a drawing; learn why a cabinetmaker handles a piece of wood in a certain manner before he marks it for cutting and shaping. Any beginning involves in getting your mind in tune with the object, making sure that all is present and ready for working, and, in our case, how best to present it in a pleasing manner.

Drop a card face down on the table. Now reach over with one hand and turn it over so it's face up. Did you turn it sideways, or lengthwise? Would one way look better than the other? Would it be dramatically better to delay the showing of the face until the last split second? Should you use your whole hand, or just the first two fingers to do the move? Which fits best with the way you've handled the

WHEN YOU DO MAGIC

cards up to now? What is the next move you have to do, and **how is the best way** to get from here to that position?

There's more to the simple move of turning a card face up than is apparent, isn't there?

What about your other actions? How do you give the deck to someone else? How do you take it back? How do you remove something from your pocket, and how do you put it away? How do you move an object from one spot to another on the table? How do you ask for the helping hand of spectator?

Learn to analyze every little move you make as you're putting a routine together. As you progress, the process will become easier and more automatic so it will eventually become second nature to you. Keep analyzing; keep looking at the table top and try to see it the same way your audiences will; keep in mind the thought that what you do isn't as important as how you do it. Will you please your audiences? Will they like what they see? Will you always be putting your best foot forward? Do these sound like a lot of probably unnecessary questions? Well, they're not!

The problem is that most amateur magicians are dull to watch because they don't have any life in them. It seems as though they believe that cards and paddles and gimmicks will automatically make a magician into an entertainer. Not so! You have to work to be an entertainer. Even the so-called naturals of show business WORK at their specialties. The fact that it seems to be effortless is proof of how hard they've worked.

Regardless of your style of magic, you have to move in order to affect your audience in a positive manner. When you don't move for periods of time is when their interest begins to lag. Since you're working close-up instead of on a stage, you're limited as to the amount of moving you can do, but only in the distances traveled.

When working, have your hands travel from one position to another in rounded movements. They should flow from one movement into the next without any jerky corners or sharp actions. They'll be easier to watch and understand, and a smooth flow makes them look graceful. Also, when your hands move from one spot to another on the tabletop, do so in a slight curve. Nature, very rarely, produces a straight line, so, psychologically, a straight movement is jarring and, therefore, very strong. To keep making straight-line movements is to continually push at the sensitivity of your audience. Save the direct moves for strengthening the finish of the trick.

To add emphasis to a move, add a small gesture at its finish. If you're drawing attention to a coin, have your hand travel to the coin, and then tap it once. If you're asking a question, time the move of your palm-down hand so the move and your question end at the same time, then turn your palm upwards.

Everything you do has a meaning; facial expressions, hand gestures, body positions-all mean something to the people who are watching you. So, again, analyze what you're doing and what you want to convey. Are the two of them in agreement, or are you sending a conflicting signal?

"Pointing" is the show business term for signaling that something is important, but without verbally telling your audience to remember it. In other words, a certain action or spoken phrase is slightly accented to make it memorable. Later, when you reach the climax, the remembered action or phrase strengthens the finish by reminding your audience of the previous problem or point.

TIMING

Timing helps to strengthen the pointing that you do if you change the speed of your working as you approach the climax. A very few times you will speed up to the finish, but usually you only do that if you are uncovering a number of surprises at the same time. You have to let your audience catch up with you visually and mentally before you show the big climax.

Timing is also important in your overall show. For example, you can do your first trick at a normal speed and the next trick at a faster speed but slow to a normal tempo as you approach the finish. Now you can do a slower trick than the first two in order to build a certain amount of drama into the plot.

As you can see, you keep your audience moving mentally. You keep changing the pace to keep their interest up, because if you keep working at the same speed you will become boring.

Watch the top people in show business and see how they constantly vary their pace and tempo. Listen to how they vary their voice and its timbre. See how they move to point up an action here, and don't move here so they don't detract from the speech or a bit of action. All of this pointing is done, in the right spots, to ensure understanding, to add surprise now or later, to sustain laughter, to build suspense, or to develop additional punch to the finish. All of them are tools that you can also use.

PERSONALITY

Personality is what makes magic work. Two magicians can do identical effects, and if one of them is a dolt, that version falls flat, regardless of how good his routine is. Those elusive qualities of humor, intelligence, caring, attitude, and other human characteristics, are mixed in varying degrees in all of us. Keith Clark (1908-1979), a very classy and successful nightclub magician, considered the voice the most important ingredient of one's personality.

"If the room is completely dark," he maintained, "you can still tell the personality by the voice." If not completely true, it is close enough. The voice is certainly important, and it can be manipulated even easier than the fingers. Look at the spells that a radio actor can weave, and we know that the actor's personality isn't like the character being played.

If you're honest with yourself, you already have a good idea of your basic personality because we all try to project ourselves in a certain way to other people. We all have varying mixtures of good and bad traits, plus our own philosophies and prejudices that become evident to our audiences. Pick the ones that will build a simple character for you to use for your shows. You can usually make changes to create what you consider a better entity, but don't try to change too many, or try to change them too much. Remember that these traits are the result of your everyday living for many years and are second nature to you.

Humor is probably the most important part of that personality that you're going to put before your audiences. Each of us has a different style of humor, and once you know your type, then the lighter side of the personality retains believability because none of the humor is forced. It's so easy to use proper grammar, but if you're not sure, ask around until you can find a friend who will know. Write down your patter (what you want to say as you do a trick), exactly as you say it, and have it corrected. When you find something in their critique that you don't understand, ask why it should be done that way. Then, when you realize what the mistake is, you won't repeat it in the future.

And, please, drop the words "right?", "Okay?" and "all right?" from the ends of your sentences. These tacked-on and completely unnecessary inquiries seem to become code words to people who don't really hear what they're saying. The use of one or more of these phrases will quickly set up a situation where the spectator addressed is required to reply, and he may not always give you the answer you want! If you say, "So I put the Four of Hearts into the center of the deck, right?", you psychologically create a challenge in the spectators' minds. They aren't sure either that it's really the Four of Hearts, or that it really went into the center of the deck. So avoid the possibility of having someone say, "No, it's still on top of the deck," by getting rid of those dangerous and superfluous endings.

LEARNING MORE

Once a person becomes interested in magic, they find that there are a lot of books, pamphlets, magazine articles, videotapes, and other sources of tricks that are available. All large cities have one or more magic shops and, usually, a magic club. So if this book sparks your interest in learning more magic, it's available out there.

Books are your best buy in magic. For the same amount of money that you can spend on one trick, you can buy a book with twenty or more tricks in it. You'll not only find three tricks that you'll want to do, but you'll be learning more about the variety and content of magic. Some magicians specialize in only one type of conjuring: cards, coins, ropes, mind-reading, balls, or even silk handkerchiefs, but it always pays to learn all you can about all the branches of magic. You never know when you can use a principle from one type of trick and apply it to one from a different specialty.

Books on magic are not only available in all magic shops, but also in most bookstores and, of course, in most libraries. So it doesn't matter what your budget is, you can find more information somewhere. Many magicians have good-sized libraries of conjuring and some have very large ones. These may include copies that have been printed as far back as the 1600s. There may only be three to six copies of that book still in existence and each one will cost thousands of dollars per copy. Most magic books from 1950 until now are still available at reasonable prices so you can make your library as complete as you wish on any of the many conjuring subjects.

At first it will be best to get general works on magic: Any title written by Bill Severn, for example:

Big Book of Magic, Guide to Magic As a Hobby, Impromptu Magic, Magic Across the Table, Magic in Your Pocket, More Magic in Your Pockets

The Magic Workshop. CompleteIllustrated Book of Card Magic by Walter Gibson, Doubleday, 1969.

Encyclopedia of Card Tricks by Jean Hugard, Dover Publications, (various editions).

Learn Magic by Henry Hay, Garden City Publishing Co., 1947.

Modern Coin Magic by J.B. Bobo, (various editions).

Royal Road to Card Magic by Jean Hugard & Fred Braue, (various editions).

200 Magic Tricks Anyone Can Do by Blackstone, Citadel Press Books, 1999

HOUDINI'S SCHOOL OF MAGIC

MAGIC WITH ANYTHING

Back in the 1700s and 1800s, it was considered socially imperative for a gentleman to know at least three or four bits of magic. This was to make him a more interesting personality at the dinner table, which was the leading social event of the day. If he could perform a couple of tricks, or "diversions" as they were called, then he was the gentleman he seemed to be.

Today it's no different. If you can do some personal entertaining, then you're one of the more desirable people to be invited to dinners and parties-provided you don't overdo it and bore everyone.

We will show you how to do first-class tricks, some of which will even intrigue and entertain amateur and professional magicians. Nothing better can happen to a magician than to see a new trick. Just because these tricks are printed in this book, don't think that all the magicians will know them, as we plan to give you a couple that are incredible!

None of the following tricks require sleight of hand, although they all have to be practiced in order to work smoothly when you present them. So, relax, turn the pages, and start your adventures as a new magician.

ASBESTOS HANDKERCHIEF

EFFECT: One of your friends has just lit a cigarette and you ask to borrow a handkerchief. Draping the cloth over your left hand, you take the cigarette and press the lit end into the center of the handkerchief and hold it there. Everyone expects a hole to be burned through the cloth but nothing happens. You hand back the cigarette, brush a couple of ashes off the cloth, and give back the handkerchief, completely undamaged.

SECRET: You have a quarter or half-dollar hidden under the handkerchief to carry away the heat from the cigarette.

PROPS NEEDED: A large coin like a quarter or half-dollar, a pocket handkerchief, which can be borrowed, a lit cigarette, which should be borrowed.

PREPARATION: Have the coin in a pocket that you can easily reach.

ROUTINE: 1. When you see your friend start to remove a pack of cigarettes, secretly get the quarter or half-dollar into your left hand. Remove your hand from your pocket and hold it in a natural position with the coin resting on the inside of your fingers.

2. After the cigarette is glowing, ask to borrow a handkerchief as you have something very interesting to show everyone. Take the hank in your right hand and drape it over your left hand, adjusting the coin underneath so it lies in the center of your palm.

3. Now take the cigarette and press the lit end right against the cloth and down onto the coin. Hold it there for at least five seconds and then hand the cigarette back. The quarter absorbs and dissipates the heat from the cigarette and prevents the handerchief from being burned or scorched.

4. Brush off the few ashes then take one corner of the handkerchief and give it back, letting your left hand with the coin fall to your side in a natural position. As the cloth is examined for a burnt hole, you can casually put your hand in your pocket to get rid of the coin.

THE RING THING

EFFECT: You borrow a solid bracelet from a lady and put your two first fingers inside of it. You revolve your fingers so the bracelet runs around and around and suddenly, when you bring your fingertips and thumbs together, the bracelet falls free with your fingertips still touching.

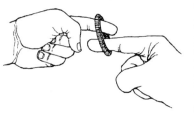

SECRET: There's a quick, secret move that no one sees.

PROPS NEEDED: A solid bracelet

ROUTINE: Revolve the bracelet around your two fingers until your

MAGIC WITH ANYTHING

right finger is at the bottom of the bracelet. Immediately do the following moves in one smooth motion:
1. Bring the tip of your thumb of each hand to the tip of the first finger.

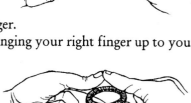

2. Swing the bracelet sideways, bringing your right finger up to your left thumb.
3. Push the tip of your first finger onto the tip of the thumb of your opposite hand.

4. Now separate the finger and thumb of each hand, and the bracelet will fall off. The beauty of this trick is that when the spectators try to do it and finish with their fingers and thumbs in the same position as when you finish, the bracelet is still trapped.

IMPORTANT POINT: You have to practice this move so that it happens in about a half a second, but smoothly. It's the smoothness of the motion that makes the trick so deceptive.

GHOSTLY GLASS

EFFECT: Taking a length of thread, you tie a large loop in one end so it fits around a drinking glass. The other end is tied loosely around the center of a wooden pencil. You hold the glass near someone's ear and have him or her ask the spirits a question. Surprisingly, the spirits apparently answer by making the glass ring softly, once for no and twice for yes.

PROPS NEEDED: A wooden pencil, a spool of heavy thread, a water tumbler, one with the mouth larger than its base

SECRET: Actually you're the one answering the questions because you control the light rings

63

coming from the glass. By slowly twisting the wooden pencil in your hand you can easily make the glass ping once or twice. You have to use strong thread and not string, as the string will soak up the miniature waves of force sent along its length from slipping on the paint of the pencil.

IMPORTANT POINTS: Make sure to use a wooden pencil and a glass that has a flared mouth so it doesn't slip out of the loop of thread.

IT'S MATCHIC

EFFECT: You place two wooden matches on the table in front of you, about a foot apart. After placing your open left hand on top of the left match, your right hand picks up the right-hand match and puts it into the left hand, which closes over it. The right hand now picks up the remaining match, and closes. When you open the left hand, it's empty. The right hand now rolls out the two matches.

PROPS NEEDED: Two wooden matches from a pocket box of matches

ROUTINE: 1. Put the two matches on the table in front of you with the heads of the matches away from you. Place your open left hand on top of the left match.

2. Pick up the match on the right by the head with your first finger and thumb and bring it to your left hand. Touch the head of the match to the base of your left fingers and close your left fingers as your right hand moves back to the right, still holding the match.

3. As your empty left hand moves away from the remaining match, your right thumb and finger let their match fall secretly onto your curved fingers.

4. Now bring your right hand over, pick up the head of the tabled matc between your first finger and thumb, and close your fingers around it as both fists are rested on the table about a foot apart.

5. Shake your left fist a little then open it to show it empty. Wait a moment, then shake your right fist and open it

MAGIC WITH ANYTHING

to roll the two matches onto the table.
IMPORTANT POINTS: As we said, the thing that really sells this trick is the steady tempo. Don't feel guilty about the hidden match in your right hand. Just let your fingers naturally relax when you reach forward to pick up the second match.

MATCHBOOK MINDREADING

EFFECT: While your back is turned, someone writes his or her initials on the insde of a matchbook. It's then closed and put on the table with two other matchbooks. When you turn around, you close your eyes, pick up each matchbook, and hold it to your head. Finally, you push one of them to the person who did the writing and when they open the book there are their initials.
PROPS NEEDED: Three matchbooks, a pen or pencil
SECRET: You have three matchbooks in your pocket and each one has been firmly, but not tightly, closed.
ROUTINE: 1. Arrange the three matchbooks in a row in front of someone. Give that person a pencil and tell them that while you turn your head that they're to pick up any matchbook and lightly write their initials inside the cover. The packet is then closed and put back down on the table.
2. When you turn back around, pick up one of the matchbooks and as you lift it to your forehead, you gently push up on the front cover

with your thumb. One of the three covers will be much looser than the other two and that is the one with the initials in it. When they closed the cover they didn't push it as firmly closed as you did, so you will be able to tell the difference when you push on it.

PENCIL PENETRATION EFFECT

EFFECT: Draping a handkerchief over your left fist, you then poke a well into it. You pick up a pencil, put it point first into the well, and proceed to push it all the way through the handkerchief and your fist,

pulling it out the bottom. You return the pencil and the handkerchief and both are unharmed.
PROPS NEEDED: A full-sized wooden pencil, a handkerchief
SECRET: It's all in the way you make the well in the handkerchief.
ROUTINE: 1. Hold one side of a borrowed handkerchief in your right hand and close your left hand into a loose fist with your thumb at the top.
2. Drape the center of the handkerchief over your fist and then, with your right thumb, poke a pocket into the cloth and down into your fist.
3. While your right hand is still over your left, open your left fist to let the pocket open all the way through your hand, and close your thumb and first finger into a circle so when you remove your right hand it still looks as though there is only a pocket in the handkerchief.

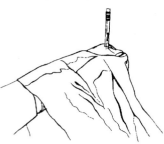

4. Pick up a pencil, put its point down into your left fist, and hold it in place by clamping it with your thumb. When you're ready, push on the eraser end of the pencil (acting as if you have to push real hard to get it through the cloth) so that it goes all the way through your fist and falls out the bottom.
5. With your right hand, pick up one of the corners of the handkerchief, shake it out to show that there isn't any hole in it, and hand it back to whomever you borrowed it from.

TWICE AS GOOD

EFFECT: While you're talking to a friend on the telephone, tell them that you're going to show them something that's twice as good. When they ask what you're talking about, tell them to get out their calculator. They are to punch in their favorite three-digit number, which can be the total of their and their spouse's ages, the first three digits of their Social Security number, or whatever. Now, they multiply that three-digit number by 13, and multiply that answer by 7, and multiply the final answer by 11. There, on the calculator screen will be their original three-digit number twice.

MAGIC WITH ANYTHING

"Now isn't that," you say, "twice as good as your original number?"
PROPS NEEDED: A pocket or desk calculator
SECRET: What you've done is make them multiply their original number by 1,001, which, of course, prints out as their number twice. The factors of 7, 11, and 13, multiply out to 1,001 so that the trick takes a little longer and the real answer is a little more obscure.

SPOTS OR NO SPOTS?

EFFECT: Remove two matches from a book of matches (wooden matches won't work) and draw a large spot in the center of each one. Holding them between the tips of your left finger and thumb, you take the matches by the finger and thumb of your right hand, turn them over, and your audience can see that the other sides of the matches are blank. You turn them over again to bring the spotted sides up, but when you turn them again you now have spots on both sides. Then all the spots vanish and you wind up with spots on just one side.
PROPS NEEDED: A book of paper matches, a pen or pencil
SECRET: The magic here is accomplished with a very simple, but undetectable, twist. As you turn the matches over with your right hand, your thumb and first finger can twist the two matches so they turn over at the same time. Because the matches have actually been turned over twice, you'll be showing the same side a second time. This way you can apparently show either spots on both sides or both sides blank.
PREPARATION: Check the matches in a lot of matchbooks until you find one where both sides of the match are almost the same color. You won't find a perfect duplicate, but close is good enough. This is because part of the match will be showing on each side of your finger and thumb and if the color difference is great, your audience will probably notice that you're not really turning the matches over.

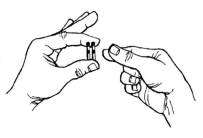

ROUTINE: 1. Take the packet of matches out of your pocket, open it, and tear out two matches. With a pen or pencil make a large spot in the center of each match on one side only. If there is a large difference in the color of the two sides, then put the spot on the second match on the opposite side of the first one.
2. Put the matches between the tips of your thumb and first finger of

your left hand so the two spots are on top. "Look," you say, "I have spots on this side."

3. Put the tip of your right thumb on top of the spots and the tip of your right first finger on the bottom of the two matches. Take the matches away from your left fingers, turn your right hand over, and put the matches back between your left finger and thumb. Take away your right hand. "And no spots on this side."

4. Turn the matches over again and show them. "Remember, we have spots on this side."

5. Take the matches in the right hand and as you turn them over, twist them between the tips of your thumb and first finger. Put them back between your left fingers. "And spots on this side."

6. Take the matches and turn them over legitimately. "So there are no spots on this side."

7. Turn the matches again with the double move. "And this side doesn't have any spots."

8. Turn the matches legitimately and show them. "Therefore, there are spots on this side."

9. Take the matches and turn them over. "And no spots on this side."
At this point you can give the matches to someone to inspector just drop them on the table.

STRAW THROUGH

EFFECT: You wrap two straws around each other in a tight knot then pull them right through each other.

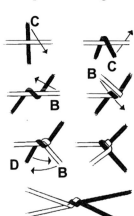

PROPS NEEDED: Two paper or plastic straws

SECRET: It's all in the way you wrap them together.

ROUTINE: 1. Put one straw on the table in front of you so it's vertical to you and lay the other one across it horizontally. Put your finger where the two straws cross and push down to flatten them.

2. With your other hand take the outer end of the vertical straw (C) and bend it toward you and slightly to the right.

3. Bend it again and push C under the right side of the horizontal straw and up slightly to the right.

4. Now bend the right end of the horizontal straw (B) diagonally to the left, making sure that you bend it in the right spot so that it looks as though it's going around the other straw.
5. Now bend B down and under the other straw.
6. Swing the lower end of the vertical straw (D) to the right and swing B to the left.
7. Holding the two ends of each straw in each hand, pull them apart.

ODD OR EVEN

EFFECT: The digits from 1 to 9 are written on a file card and then the card is torn into nine pieces, one digit to each piece. The pieces are mixed by anyone and then placed under a napkin. Putting your hands under the cloth, you work with the pieces for a less than a minute. When you bring your hands out from under the napkin, one of them holds only the even numbers and the other holds only the odd ones.

PROPS NEEDED: A blank, white "3 x 5" file card, a pen or pencil, a cloth napkin or handkerchief
SECRET: Because of the way you've written the numbers and torn the card all of the pieces with the odd numbers will have two straight edges (except for the 5, which will have four rough edges) and all of the even numbers will have one straight edge.

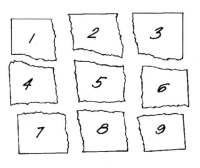

ROUTINE: 1. Write the digits on the card so you have them in three rows of three numbers each.
2. When you're done, tear the card into three pieces by tearing it from top to bottom, and then tear each of those pieces into thirds. DO NOT put any pieces together and tear them together as the edges will tear too smoothly.
3. Give the nine pieces to someone to mix in their hands and then put the pieces under a napkin.
4. Under the napkin, pick up any piece and run the tip of your first finger along all four edges. If it has only one smooth edge, put it into your left hand. If it has two or more smooth edges, then keep it in the fingers of your right hand.

5. Pick up another piece, feel the edges, and if it has one smooth edge, put in your left hand. If not, then keep it in your right.
6. Go through all the pieces, separating them as you go.
7. Open your left hand and tell your audience that it has all of the even numbers. Drop them in a pile on the table.
8. Say that the other hand has all of the odd numbers and drop them on the table in a second pile so someone can verify them.
9. As soon as you can, pick up all the pieces and dump them before someone starts comparing the torn edges.

PENETRATING MATCHES

EFFECT: You hold a wooden match between the tips of your thumb and second finger of each hand so each match is trapped within the circle of the other hand. By moving your hands so the matches bump against each other, you show that the matches are not only trapped, but are also very solid.

"Watch!" you say. "One, two, three..."

The instant you say three, pull your two hands apart and the matches apparently penetrate each other.

PROPS NEEDED: Two wooden matches

SECRET: You can even do this trick fairly slowly and the spectators still won't see how it works. As you're setting up the trick by putting the matches between the tips of your fingers, you push constantly on the ends of the matches. As you continue to talk move both thumbs slightly away from the tips of the second fingers. One, or both, of the matches will stick to either your thumb or your finger. That's the match that will do the magic.

ROUTINE: Holding the matches firmly between the tips of your fingers, tell your audience to watch closely. Slowly count to three. On the count of three you do three things:
1. Rotate your hands so the back of one hand is toward the eyes of your spectators.
2. Move the non-magic match toward the end of the magic match (the one that will separate from your finger) and open a small gap at the end of the magic match.
3. Move the non-magic match through the opening between the magic

match and your finger, close the gap, and then rotate your hands back to the original position.

At this point, if you want to repeat the trick, drop the non-magic match and set it up again between the tips of your fingers so the two matches are trapped. You're now all set to repeat the routine.

THE CLASSIC COIN AND GLASS

EFFECT: A borrowed coin is put on the table and covered with a glass that is wrapped with paper to make it opaque. You intend to make the coin penetrate the table, but it doesn't work the first time you try it. You try again then get exasperated and smash the glass. The paper crumples, the glass is gone, everyone hears the coin drop into the glass, and you bring the glass out from under the table with the coin inside.

PROPS NEEDED: A coin, a water glass, a half-sheet of newspaper

SECRET: You actually steal the glass out of its paper shell when no one suspects and it's all a matter of timing and a good routine.

PREPARATION: You need a duplicate of the coin you intend to borrow, a glass tumbler, and half of a page of newspaper. Shortly before you plan to do the trick, get your coin (let's say it's a quarter) and secretly set it on your right knee.

ROUTINE: 1. If you're at a dinner table, make sure the glass is dry before you use it.

2. Fold the half-page of newspaper as shown and roll the glass into it. Twist the paper at the bottom of the glass then set the glass upside down on the table to your right.

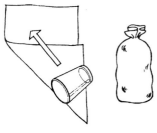

3. Ask for the loan of a quarter and place it on the table about foot in front of you. Carefully cover the coin with the wrapped glass and look at your audience.

4. "This is going to be very difficult," you tell your audience, "so I'd like you to watch closely, but very quietly. I'm going to try to pull the coin right through the wood of the table."

5. Lean forward and put your left hand under the table as you steady the glass with your right hand. Drum your first left two fingers against the bottom of the tabletop, then make two more taps, and then one. Straighten up, but leave your left hand in your lap.

"I'm not sure. It either got stuck halfway through, or it didn't go at all."
6. Lift the glass with your right hand and bring it past the edge of the table so your right wrist is resting on the edge.
7. As you bend forward to look at the coin still on the table, let the glass drop quietly into your left hand. Shake your head and gently put the paper shell back over the coin, keeping it in place with your right hand. "I'll try again," you say.
8. As your left hand goes under the table again it takes the glass and puts it between your knees. Again, your left fingers drum a pattern on the table. There's a short wait and you drum again.
9. "Awww, it's not going to work!" you say and you smash your right hand down on the paper shell.
10. Wait a second, then your left fingers drop your coin into the glass so it makes a clink. You slowly bring the glass out in your left hand and put it on the table as your right hand drags the paper back toward you so the borrowed coin drops into your lap. You then toss the paper aside and everything can be examined.
IMPORTANT POINTS: If all the glasses at the table have too much liquid in them, you can use a salt shaker in place of the glass. You won't need as much newspaper, either. You can also use paper napkins to wrap the shaker, but make sure they're large ones. Avoid using bar napkins, as you have to fight to keep them together while you're doing the trick.

A HEAVY COIN

EFFECT: Someone puts a coin into the center of a napkin while you hold a glass in your hand. They then grasp the coin through the napkin and turn it upside down, bringing the covered coin right over the opening of the glass. You have the person drop the coin and everyone hears it fall into the glass. Putting the glass on a book, you hold the book in one hand and tap the top of the napkin with the other hand. Suddenly the coin drops through the book and glass and onto the table. When the napkin is taken away, the coin, naturally, is gone.

To prove that even magicians sometimes have a difficult time, the glass is filled halfway with water and again put on top of the book you're holding. You cover the glass with the napkin, and hold it out toward someone.
"Just lift the glass off the book," you say.

MAGIC WITH ANYTHING

They reach out, lift the glass, and will then look at you to find out why it should be difficult.

The glass is put back on the book, the napkin removed, and someone holds the coin in the center of the upside down napkin. They put the napkin over the glass so the coin is again just above the edge of the glass.

"Drop the coin into the glass."

Again, everyone hears the coin fall into the glass.

"Everyone knows you can't compress a liquid, but I didn't know that liquid will increase mass. The water in the glass will affect the weight of the coin. Here, lift the glass."

Someone tries picking up the covered glass and can't. It simply refuses to be lifted off the book.

You remove the napkin, put the book at the edge of a table, and slide the glass off onto the top of it.

"Light may have something to do with it," you say as you easily pick up the glass and pour the water and coin out into a dish.

PROPS NEEDED: A coin, a water glass, water for the glass, a handkerchief or cloth napkin, a hardbound book

SECRET: You actually have two separate tricks here, blended into one routine. Your left hand under the napkin manipulates the glass both times.

ROUTINE: 1. Set up your props as described in the beginning of the effect and just before you have the person drop the coin into the glass, secretly tip the glass toward you. The way the napkin spreads out over the glass will give you plenty of space to maneuver so no one suspects that the glass is at an angle.

2. The coin will hit the side of the glass and slide into your fingers.

3. Straighten the glass as your other hand reaches for the book. Place the glass on top of the book and hold the book with the hand that has the coin. Hold the book with your fingers underneath and your thumb on top, next to the glass.

4. When you tap the top of the glass with your other hand, your fingers let the coin drop onto the table. Remove the napkin to show

that the coin is no longer in the glass.

5. Fill the glass about halfway with water, put the glass on the book, pick up the book with your fingers underneath and your thumb on top, and cover the glass with the napkin.

6. Ask someone to lift the glass and they'll do it quite easily.

7. Remove the napkin, have someone put the coin back in the center, and then hold them over the glass.

8. Tell them to drop the coin into the glass.

9. While you're asking someone to lift the glass, your first finger comes out from under the book, and you squeeze the base of the glass between your finger and thumb. Amazingly, just those two fingers can keep anyone from lifting the glass from the book.

10. Just before you remove the napkin your finger goes back under the book and everything is just the same as before. Slide the glass off onto the table and let your spectators wonder.

SLIDE FOR LIFE

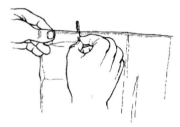

EFFECT: You pin a safety pin through the hem of a handkerchief and have the owner hold the two corners on each side of the pin. Taking hold of the end of the pin, you magically slide the pin all the way to one corner without tearing the cloth!
PROPS NEEDED: A safety pin at least 1 1/2" long, and a handkerchief.
SECRET: It's all in the way you hold the pin, but it certainly looks and sounds scary.

ROUTINE: 1. Have the owner of the handkerchief hold two adjacent corners of it and you pin the safety pin through the cloth, just to the left of the center and just under the hem.

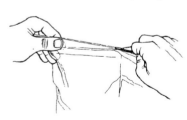

2. Your left hand takes hold of the hem to the left of the pin and you push the pin back and forth through the cloth to show everyone that it really is pinned.

3. Now exert a little pull to your left with your left hand so the hem is in an absolutely straight line to the right, as your right hand turns the pin horizontal so the head is to

MAGIC WITH ANYTHING

your left. Now, if you pull the pin directly to the right, the cloth will slip between the tip of the pin and the head.

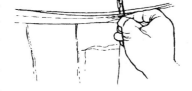

4. Stop when you get to the right corner, quickly turn the pin so it's aimed directly away from you, and push the point of the pin back through the cloth.
It now looks as if the bar of the pin magically penetrated the cloth of the handkerchief.

CATCH IT

EFFECT: Using a long necklace you make two loops on the table, and challenge anyone to put their finger in the center of the loop so that when you pull on the two ends of the necklace their finger will be caught in the center. It seems that they're successful only when you want them to be.
PROPS NEEDED: A necklace or chain at least 36" long when it's doubled
SECRET: It's all in the way you coil the necklace as you lay it out on the table.
Pattern One: Hold the two ends of the necklace together and pull the center out as far as it will go so the two strands of the necklace are together. Make sure that neither strand crosses over the other. Curl the center back around into a spiral, keeping the strands flat on the table, and slightly spread the center into an open loop. Pick up strand #3 and bring it over strand #2 to place it next to strand #1. Now slide #2 up next to #4 and open both loops A and B with your fingers.
If someone puts a finger into loop A, the finger will be caught. But, if the finger is in loop B, the necklace will come free

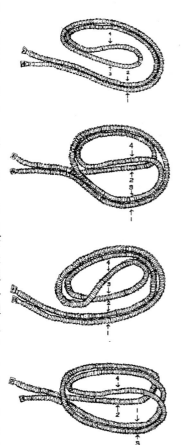

when you pull on its two ends.

Pattern Two: Make the coil in exactly the same way, but let one strand cross over the other just before you finish making the coil. Again, put strand #3 over #2 and slide it up to #1, then push #2 up to #4. Open up the two loops.

This time, neither loop will catch a finger put in the center. So, this is a no-win pattern.

ROUTINE: 1. Start by making Pattern One, put your finger into loop A, pull on the two ends, and show that the necklace catches on your fingers. Tell them that this is a winning move.

2. Make Pattern One again and invite someone to put a finger into either loop. Pull on the ends to show the result.

3. Make Pattern Two three times in a row so no one wins. Then make Pattern One, put your finger in loop A, and show that the necklace will catch a finger.

13¢ OF MINDREADING
(Bob Hummer)

EFFECT: Two nickels and three pennies are put on the table in no particular pattern. You turn your back and someone turns over one coin at a time, saying "Turn," each time, until they want to go through the second step. At that point, they either turn over all of the pennies or all of the nickels, but without saying anything. They now resume turning over single coins, saying "Turn," each time, until they decide they're done. When you turn back around you tell them whether they turned over the nickels or the pennies.

PROPS NEEDED: Two nickels and three pennies

ROUTINE: 1. Either you can put the coins on the table or have someone else do it. Explain that while your back is turned anyone can turn a coin over so the opposite side is up, to say "Turn" as they do so, and they can keep doing this as long as they want.

2. As you're explaining this, quickly count how many coins are showing their heads side up. If there aren't any heads showing, consider that as a count of zero. Now turn around and have them start turning over coins. Every time you hear them say "Turn," add one to your mental total.

3. When they decide to stop, tell them to turn over either all three of the pennies or all of the nickels, but not to say anything.

4. Now they start turning over single coins again, saying "Turn," and

MAGIC WITH ANYTHING

you continue your count. When they've stopped the second time, turn around and count the number of tails showing.

5. Add that number to your total. If the answer is odd, then they turned over all of the nickles; if the answer is even, then they turned over all of the pennies.

For example, let's say that you counted three heads before you turned your back. They called out "Turn" four times before they stopped, so you add three and four to get a total of seven. The second time they turned over coins they called out "Turn" two more times, so seven plus two makes nine. When you turn around let's say that there are four tails showing; adding nine and four gives you thirteen, an odd number. Therefore, they turned over all of the nickels.

INTERLUDE WITH A KNIFE

EFFECT: Four small pieces of paper are moistened and stuck onto the blade of a table knife, two on each side. The pieces are shown again, two on each side, and the pieces are then removed two at a time, and showing both sides of the knife each time. When the knife blade is empty on both sides, a magic wave is made in the air, from left to right, and two of the pieces come back onto the blade. Another wave and the other two pieces come back. Now a wave is made in the opposite direction and two of the pieces vanish by themselves.

PROPS NEEDED: A paper napkin. A table knife, preferably a butter knife with a rounded tip. A glass of water

PREPARATION: The only preparation to this trick is that you have to learn to do what is called a Paddle Move to make it work. This move apparently lets you show both sides of the knife when, in reality, you show the same side twice.

Hold the knife in front of you with the blade pointing straight out and with your hand palm up. Turn your hand so the blade swivels up and back toward you in order to show the other side, but give the handle a half-twist at the same time. Now, with the knife blade pointing at you and your knuckles upwards, it looks as if you're showing the other

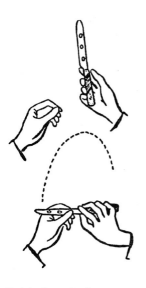

side of the knife, but it's still the first side. Turn your hand back down so it's palm upwards again, twisting the knife as you do so, and it looks as though you're showing the first side again.

To actually show both sides of the knife do the same moves, but without twisting the knife. Both moves have to look exactly the same to your audience. Do NOT lift your hand as you turn the knife over, merely twist your wrist so your arm doesn't move up and down.

ROUTINE: 1. Take a corner of the napkin and tear off four squares of paper about a half inch square, moisten each one, and stick them to the blade of the knife so there are two on each side, about two inches apart, and so that each square is in the same position as a square on the opposite side.

2. Show your audience, which has been watching all along, that you now have two pieces of paper on this side (holding the knife with the blade pointing away from you), and two more pieces on the other side (and you turn the knife over). Turn it back to show the first side again.

3. With your left thumb cover the piece closer to you on the knife and pull it off the knife. Make sure that the tip of your first finger (which is on the bottom of the blade) doesn't pull off the piece on that side. Drop your left hand to your side and pretend to drop the piece of paper, and then bring your left hand up to the same level as the knife and slightly to the left of it.

4. Now apparently turn the knife over (actually making the paddle move) at the same time that you bring your left hand to the knife. Cover the blank spot (where you just removed the paper) with either your first finger or your thumb, depending on which one has the paper stuck to it. Apparently pull off the piece of paper at that position, show it, and then drop your hand to get rid of it. Drop the knife back to the first position, again making the paddle move.

5. This time remove the outer piece of paper with your left thumb, and repeat all the moves again.

6. After you've apparently removed the second set of pieces, apparently show both sides of the knife to show it blank by doing the paddle move as you turn it over.

7. Now make a clockwise circle in the air with the knife and twist it between your fingers so the second side comes up on top. You now have two pieces of paper on top.

8. Turn the knife over, without making the paddle move, to show that the second side is still empty. Bring the knife back to the first position.

9. Make another clockwise circle in the air, and do the paddle move to

show that the second set of paper pieces has also come back.
10. Now make a counterclockwise circle in the air, and turn the knife over to show that the second set has vanished. Wipe the two pieces of paper off the one side of the blade, and you're done.

BEHEADED MATCH
(Fred Peterson)

EFFECT: One match is torn out of a paper book of matches, and given to someone to examine, and mark, if they wish. As you take back the match, your helper holds out both hands, open and with the palm upwards. The head is torn off the match and put on their right hand and the stem of the match is put on their left hand, which closes over it. Picking up the head of the match, you make it vanish by hitting it against the back of their closed hand. When they open their fingers, the match is restored to its original condition.
PROPS NEEDED: A book of matches
PREPARATION: Beforehand you've removed a match from the booklet that you plan to use in the trick, twisted off the head of the match, and put the head in your left pocket. Just before you start the trick, get the head between the first and second fingers of your left hand, so it's squeezed between the first joints of those fingers.
ROUTINE: 1. Open the packet of matches and tear out one match. Give it to one of your spectators, and ask her to examine it. Tell her that she can also write her initials on it if she wishes. When she's satisfied that it's an ordinary match, take it back with your right first finger and thumb, and so that the head is pointing to your left.
2. Now, as you ask her to hold out both hands so they're both open and with her palms upward, you drop your right hand about a foot and use your right middle finger to rotate the match so its head is now to your right.
3. Bring your two hands together in front of your so your left first finger and thumb cover the bare end of the match, and your right fingers hide the head. Twist both hands as though you're tearing off the head of the match, and then drop the match head from your left fingers onto her right hand.
4. Bring the match to her left hand so it touches her palm, and ask her to hold it. Don't let go of the match until her fingers close over yours and so she can't see that the head is still on the match. Tell her to hold it tight.

HOUDINI'S SCHOOL OF MAGIC

5. Your right fingers pick up the match head, as you say, "Watch! On the count of three. . ."

6. Lift your right fingers up to the level of your head, and then bring them back down to lightly touch the back of her fist, counting "One." Repeat the move, counting "Two." When you lift your hand the third time, toss the match head behind you and immediately bring your hand down and strike her fist with your the tip of your first finger, counting "Three!"

7. Tell her to open her hand and there will be the completely restored match.

MOVING MATCHES

EFFECT: A pocket box of wooden matches is opened and the matches dumped onto the table. Four of them are picked up and placed in a row in front of you. One match is put into your left hand, and your right picks up the remaining three matches. A shake of your two fists, and when your hands are opened one of the matches has travelled from your right hand to your left. Each hand gets two matches, the fists are again shaken, and a third match travels to your left hand. The last match is picked up by your right hand and thrown invisibly toward your left fist. Your left hand shows four matches, and your right hand is shown empty.

PROPS NEEDED: A small box of wooden matches

ROUTINE: 1. Open the drawer of the matchbox and dump the matches into a pile to your left.

2. Discard the box and pick up a group of matches in your right hand.

3. Drop four of them into a row in front of you and with the heads away from you. Drop all but one of the remaining matches onto the large pile to your left, holding that secret match so its head is in the crease of the first joint of your middle finger and its other end is against the base of that finger.

4. Your right fingers pick up the match on the left of the row of four, and drop it and the secret match into your left hand, your left fingers closing over them so no one sees the second match.

5. Pick up the other three matches in your right hand so that one of them rests in that clipped position in your middle finger, and close that hand into a fist.

6. Give each fist a little shake, turn your hands so they're palm downwards, and open them. Two matches fall out of your left fist, and you let two matches fall out of your right, retaining the third match in your curved middle finger.

7. Your right hand comes to the left, picks up one match from the left pile, drops it into your open left hand, picks up the second match, and drops it and the secret match into your closing left hand.

8. Your right fingers pick up the two matches on the right, getting one into the clipped position, and closes into a fist.

9. Another shake of your fists to make the magic happen, you open your left fist to drop three matches onto the table, and your right hand lets one match fall.

10. You pick up the three matches on the left, one at a time, with your right hand and dropping its secret match into the left fist with the third one.

11. The last match on the table is picked up and put into clipped position as you again make a fist.

12. This time, you make a throwing motion toward your left fist with your right hand, opening your fingers at the same time to show that the last match has apparently left your hand and keeping your hand palm downward.

13. Immediately open your left hand to drop its four matches onto the table as the tips of your right fingers rest on the edge of the table. Let the secret match drop into your lap, and you can then lean forward and show that both hands are empty.

COFFEE CATCH

ROUTINE: Two pieces of a paper napkin are wadded up to form small balls of paper, and are covered by an upside down coffee cup. You put the fingers of one hand on the bottom of the cup and apparently pull one of the balls right through the china. Lifting the cup you show that only one ball is left, and cover it again. This time your hand goes under the table and pulls the second ball down through the wood, and you can show the cup and both hands empty.

PROPS NEEDED: A coffee cup. A paper ball made from a paper napkin matching the one you're going to use in the trick.

PREPARATION: The extra ball is in your lap.

ROUTINE: 1. Pick up a paper napkin, tear it in half, and then tear one half in half again. Take each of those quarters and wad them into a ball that matches the ball in your lap.

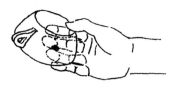

2. Use the second half of the napkin to wipe out the cup, and then drop the paper to one side as your right hand drops to your lap and picks up the secret ball. Hold it between the tips of your right first and middle fingers.

3. Pick up the cup with your left fingers inside the edge of the cup, and drop it upside down over the two balls. Just before you let the edge of the cup drop onto the table, steal one of the balls between the tips of your left first and middle fingers.

4. Hold the tips of your left fingers on the edge of the table as your

right hand comes over the top of the cup. Push the tips of all four fingers against the bottom of the cup, and as you turn your hand over your thumb roll the secret ball to the tip of your first finger. Show the ball and drop it to one side.

5. Your right hand now picks up the cup to show only one ball on the table, and then, as your hand returns the cup over that remaining ball, your right fingers steal the ball.

6. As you rest your right fingers against the edge of the table you put your left hand under the table, knock against the bottom of the table top, and bring your hand out to show a ball at the tips of your first finger and thumb. At the same time you let the ball in your right fingers drop into your lap.

7. Now you can show both hands empty.

IMPORTANT POINTS: This is a very simple trick, but will fool your audiences only if you learn to steal the balls with both hands. The fact that you alternate your two hands in magically removing the balls from under the cup keeps you one move ahead of their attention and, thus, off balance. Learn to do the entire routine in a steady one-two-three cadence so their eyes and mind have to follow what you're doing right now and not be able to get ahead of you. The fact that both hands are seen to be empty during the routine also helps you fool them as you make the moves, and they won't be able to reconstruct the trick afterwards to find any weak points.

MAGIC WITH ANYTHING

FLYING RING

EFFECT: A borrowed finger ring is held in your fist as someone fastens a handkerchief over your entire hand and fastens it in place with a rubber band. A second handkerchief or napkin is fastened around your other hand. You bump your two encased fists together and, apparently, the ring jumps right through your fingers and cloth as it's in the other hand when the handkerchiefs are removed.

PROPS NEEDED: Two handkerchiefs or cloth napkins. Two rubber bands large enough to go over your fists

ROUTINE: 1. Have all of your audience in front of you and the props on the table as you ask to borrow a finger ring.

2. Take it in your left hand, show it, and then close your fingers over it to make a fist.

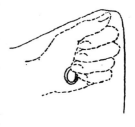

3. Pick up one of the handkerchiefs with your right hand and drape it over your fist. As you arrange the cloth so that the cloth on the audience side is slightly longer than the cloth on your side, change your grip on the ring so it's now held by the tip of your left ring finger against the base of your thumb.

4. Your right hand points to the rubber bands and as you ask someone to put one of them around your fist, gesture with your right hand. It circles your left hand from the back, up over the top, down in front, underneath, and back up to the back. But-as your right hand goes under your left fist you drop the ring so it falls down through the folds of the cloth and into your right hand as it goes by. Do not hesitate as you make this move. Your right hand has to make a continuous circle around your fist in one, smooth move.

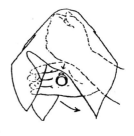

5. Your right hand slips the ring onto the tip of your ring finger so your open right hand can then gesture to the second handkerchief as you ask for it to be put around your right fist.

6. Then have the remaining rubber band put around your wrist to hold it in place.

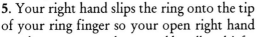

83

HOUDINI'S SCHOOL OF MAGIC

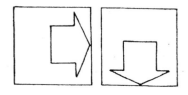

7. Bump your fists together to apparently make the magic happen, and then have your left fist undone. Show it empty, and when the hankkerchief is taken off your other hand, there is the ring.

IMPORTANT POINTS: Keep practicing the circling move with your right hand around your left until you can do it smoothly and without hesitation.

Also, when it's time to put the second handkerchief around your right hand, don't say that it's empty. Just close your hand into a fist and have the hank put around it. As soon as you say that it's empty, someone will want to see your empty hand, and you can't do that.

WHICH WAY IS UP?

EFFECT: You show a square of cardboard that has a large arrow painted on each side, and when you turn the cardboard between your fingers the two arrows point in the same direction. But whenever you snap your fingers, the arrows point in odd directions, sometimes at right angles to each other and at other times they're opposite to each other.

PROPS NEEDED: A piece of stiff cardboard two to three inches square and a black marker.

PREPARATION: With a black marker draw an arrow on the first side so that it runs from the center to the right edge. When it's finished, turn the card from left to right and draw a duplicate arrow so it starts at the center and points to the bottom of the square. In other words, the two arrows are actually at right angles to each other.

The cardboard square is easily carried in a pocket so you can pull it out and do the trick any time you like. It's especially good for children as they start thinking that the arrows can actually move around.

ROUTINE: 1. Hol
d the card between your two hands so your left fingers and thumb are at the lower left corner and your right fingers and thumb are at the upper right corner. If the card is small enough for you, then hold it with your right thumb at the lower left and your middle finger at the upper right so your left first finger can turn the card over to show the other side. In either case, the arrow should be pointing away from

you. Turn the card over two or three times and you see that both arrows point away from you.

2. Now take the card with your left fingers at the upper left corner so you can snap your right fingers to make the magic happen. But, when your right fingers again grip the card, take it at the lower right corner. Now when you turn the card over the two arrows point up and down.

3. This time you're going to do a series of very sneaky moves. Hold the card so the arrow is pointing toward you, with your left fingers still holding it at the upper left corner. Snap your right fingers and again take the lower right corner, but lift that corner so the bottom of the card pivots up and away from you. When the card is again flat, your left fingers are at the lower left corner and your right fingers are at the upper right, and the arrow is now pointing to your left.

4. Snap your right fingers, and again take the upper right corner, twist the card between the two corners, and the second arrow now points to your right.

5. Snap your fingers as your left fingers move up to the upper left corner, take hold of the lower right corner, and again do the sneaky move where you pivot the card away from you so the second arrow will point away from you.

6. Twist the card two or more times between the two corners to show that the arrows are again pointing in the same direction and you're done.

HOUDINI'S SCHOOL OF MAGIC

PLAYING WITH CARDS

We're going to start you out with some of the basic handling techniques of playing cards so you'll feel at home with them when you're presenting any of the following tricks.

Basic card handling starts with being able to keep an entire deck or a small packet of cards square in your hands; that is, that all four edges are lined up exactly from the top to the bottom. This makes it much easier to work with the cards, as there aren't any jagged edges to fight when you're cutting or shuffling the pack. You should put in a lot of practice picking up a deck of cards, dealing the cards into one, two, or three piles, and cutting the deck on the table. All of these actions should be done at a steady rate of speed, the cards should stay in neat piles, and the packet in your hand should always be squared.

If you're going to be doing card tricks and want people to think you have a good basic knowledge about playing cards, then you should be able to handle them in an expert manner. And people ARE impressed by card tricks. There is a very old book named *La Piazza Universale di tutte le professione del Mundo*, written by Th. Garzoni in Venice, Italy, in 1593. On page 565, he praises a man named M. Abramo Colorni Hebreo as knowing many card tricks. So you will be joining a very long line of distinguished personalities who are able to entertain their friends, as well as perfect strangers, with some skill and secret knowledge about playing cards.

THE MECHANIC'S GRIP

The best way to hold a deck for dealing is the Mechanic's Grip, named for the cheating card manipulators who needed a basic grip that would work for all of their card moves. It holds the deck firmly, but so the right fingers can approach and take any cards you want: the top, the second, or the bottom. The grip is also ideal for doing so many of the two-handed moves so essential for sleight of hand with cards.

The first key to the Mechanic's Grip is the position of your first and second fingers at the upper right corner of the cards. The second key is having the lower left corner firmly pressed against the ball of your thumb. Your first finger keeps the packet squared from top to bottom, pushing against the base of the thumb while your second finger squares the cards from the side, also against the base of the thumb. We can't be any more explicit than that because each person's hand is slightly different, so some experimentation is needed to find the correct position for you. You'll know when you're right because you'll be able to take all your fingers away from the cards, except the first and second, and the packet or deck will remain squared and in the correct position.

THE SPREAD

An important move for any card magician is to be able to spread the cards in a smooth line across the table. This is accomplished only with a lot of practice, even though it's a simple move to learn.

Open a new deck of cards, as it will be easier to learn with a new deck and then you'll be able to do it later with older decks. Hold the deck from 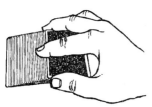 above with the middle two fingers of your right hand at the outside end and your thumb on the inner end. Place the deck to your left on a smooth tablecloth and move your first finger and middle finger to the left edge of the deck, keeping ring finger, little finger, and thumb where they are. Now spread the deck to your right, letting your first and middle fingers regulate the cards as they leave the deck and spread out on the table. By varying the pressure on the cards, you will soon learn to lay them out in a smooth, evenly spaced row.

To make an elegant spread, curve it as you bring the deck across the table in front of you. It should now be in a slight arc.

THE TURNOVER FLOURISH

This is the move that most lay people expect gamblers and magicians to be able to do, so here it is for you to learn.

Spread the deck across the table in front of you in a straight line. Carefully remove the top card with your right hand, move it to the bottom of the pack, and insert one end halfway under the bottom card. Now, using the single card as a hinged lever, lift the bottom cards of the deck and turn them over. This will create a wave in the pack and all of the cards will turn over so the deck is now face-up.

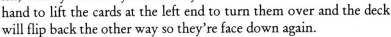

If you hold your left hand at the left end of the spread as you perform the flourish, when you finish you can use your left hand to lift the cards at the left end to turn them over and the deck will flip back the other way so they're face down again.

Quickly slide your right hand to the left and you'll gather up the entire deck in your hand ready to be squared.

THE OVERHAND SHUFFLE

Hold the deck in your right hand with one of the long edges uppermost and with the faces toward your palm, your thumb on the inner end, your last three fingers on the outer end, and your first finger resting on the upper edge. Bring your left hand to the deck, so your fingers go under the bottom edge of the deck, and use your left thumb to hold back a small group of cards from the top of the pack as your right hand lifts the deck straight up. When the deck clears that small group, they will fall onto your left fingers, and you immediately repeat the move with another small group of cards. You can continue on  through the deck by taking off from six to ten cards at a time and the deck will be shuffled.

The overhand shuffle is also good for keeping a certain group of cards on the top or bottom of the deck while giving the illusion of shuffling the deck. In this case, if you want to retain the top portion of the deck, hold the deck so the faces are toward your left. If you want to keep the bottom portion intact, hold the deck so the faces are toward your right palm. Now shuffle off groups of cards until you get about to the center of the pack and do the following move in one motion: Tip the shuffled-off cards in your left hand slightly to the left and drop the remainder of the cards that are in your right hand into your left hand, but to the right of those cards. Now turn the deck so it's face-up or facedown, square the cards, and you're ready to continue with the trick.

THE HINDU SHUFFLE

This shuffle is a variation of the way they shuffle in some parts of Europe and is very handy for certain tricks. Grasp the deck face down from below near the tips of your left fingers, with your middle two fingers on the right long edge and your thumb on the right long edge. Your right hand comes over to grip the right end of the deck,

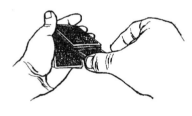

holding it the same as your left fingers, but from above. Bow your left fingers a little as your right hand pulls the majority of the lower part of the deck away from your left fingers. A small group of cards from the top of the deck will be retained by your left fingers and will then fall to your left palm when the lower part is free. If you repeat the move, more groups will be dropped into your left palm until the deck is finished.

Again, if you want to keep a certain group of cards on the top or bottom of the deck, you use the moves of the Hindu Shuffle, but while holding the deck in a certain way. Let's say you want to keep the bottom cards in order. Hold the deck facedown, as described, shuffle almost to the bottom of the deck, and slide the remainder of the cards under the cards in your left hand. Square the cards and you're ready to go.

If you want to keep the top cards intact, then do the same moves but while holding the deck face-up.

PLAYING WITH CARDS

THE RIFFLE SHUFFLE

This shuffle always looks so easy, but takes a lot practice to make it look that way. It is invaluable for controlling cards or groups of cards for certain gambling cheats or card tricks and is a further proof of you being able to handle cards like the experts.

Place the deck on the table in front of you facedown, just to the right of center, so the length of the cards runs from left to right. Hold the deck with one hand at each end, thumbs on the inner edge and the middle fingers and ring fingers on the outer edge next to the corners. Your  first fingers rest lightly on the top card and your little fingers are free.

With your left thumb, riffle up the inner left corner of the deck and stop halfway through the cards. Lift off all the cards above that break with your left hand and put them on the table to the left of the lower half. As you put the left-hand cards on the table, bring the left end slightly toward you. Your right hand angles its packet clockwise so when all the cards are on the table  the two packets are slightly separated in a V-shape at their inner ends. Keep all your fingers right where they are, but push down with your first fingers on the outer ends of the two packets. Your thumbs lift the inner edges of the two packets and continue upwards so the cards riffle downwards and mesh together at the inner corners.

Still keeping all your fingers where they are, your thumbs again grip the inner edges so you can push the two packets together in front 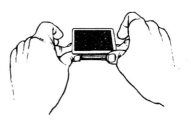 of you. The packets will stop about three-quarters of the way closed as the cards are being pinched together. Keeping your first fingers on top and your thumbs on the inner edges, move your middle fingers so they are on the outside ends.

As you push the two packets all the way together, your middle fingers and thumbs move toward each other to square the cards by squeezing the two inner corners. As you grow more proficient with the shuffle, you'll see that no one can see any of the faces of the cards and that you can learn to control a certain number of the top cards to stay on top, or most of the bottom cards to stay on the bottom, or both. The main thing to learn is to riffle the edges of the cards in one smooth motion so they will make an almost perfect interweave-that is, so the cards almost alternate from the two packets.

THREE DECKS

Although most of the tricks in this book can be done with the use of only one regular deck of playing cards, it is advisable for you to have at least three decks. You should have two matching decks of whichever color you will usually work with and one deck of a contrasting color. Some of the tricks may require one or more duplicate cards and your extra deck, which is the second deck of the same color, can provide the necessary duplicate cards and should be plainly marked on the outside of its case so you know that it is short some cards.

THE SELECTED CARD

It is very important that when someone has selected a card that you're about to conjure with, that they remember which card they have. The best way to make sure that the card isn't completely forgotten is to have the selector show the card to one or two other people. When you ask for the name of the card and the spectator doesn't remember, the others can at least vote on it and come up with the right name.

   Also, when you get to the end of the trick and are about to reveal that you've found the right card under impossible circumstances, have the spectator name the selected card BEFORE you show the one you have. First, it heightens the drama since everyone now knows which card you've been looking for, and will instantly recognize it as soon as you turn it over. Second, in the few cases (at least in the beginning) when you've found the wrong card, you now have a chance to put this card back into the deck and look for the right one. After this has happened to you a couple of times, you'll figure out how to turn a bad situation into a good one, depending on which

PLAYING WITH CARDS

trick you're doing.

To help you perfect your card handling skills, here are some tricks that will only use some simple moves. As you progress the moves will become a little more complicated, but the tricks will become much closer to veritable miracles, so all your work will be for a good cause.

PIANO CARDS

EFFECT: A spectator helps you make two piles of cards and you then make an extra card travel invisibly from one pile to another.
PROPS NEEDED: A deck of cards
SECRET: Each of the two piles is made up of odd cards because you took seven pairs of cards and divided them into two piles. Therefore, the "extra" card that you add gives that pile an even number of cards.
ROUTINE: 1. Ask someone to place their hands on the table as if they're playing a piano with their first knuckles. Push two cards off the pack saying, "Two cards," and place them between the last two fingers of their left hand.
2. Take two more cards saying, "Two more cards," and place them between the next pair of fingers.
3. Repeat the action with two cards between the next two fingers and then with a pair of cards between the thumb and first finger.
4. Now begin putting pairs of cards into their right hand, starting with the thumb/first fingers space. When you get to the last pair of fingers, however, you openly put just ONE card there.
5. Putting the deck aside, you begin taking back the pairs of cards, saying each time, "Two cards." After you pick up each pair, take one card in each hand, and drop them on the table about six inches apart, creating two piles.
6. When you get to the last single card, hold it up and ask, "On which of these two piles do you want me to put this odd card?"
7. Whichever pile they select, put the single card on it, then snap your fingers to make it jump magically to the other pile.
8. Pick up the pile that you put the single card on, and deal off the cards in pairs; it will come out even.
9. Pick up the other pile, deal off those cards in pairs onto the first

cards, and you'll finish with an odd card. Apparently the odd card has traveled from one pile to the other.

IMPORTANT POINTS: If you examine the two piles before you add the single card, you'll find an odd number of cards in each one. It's important that your audience doesn't figure this out. So, as you put the cards between their fingers you have to say each time, either, "Two cards," or "A pair of cards." You do this to keep them thinking about an even number. Again, when you take back each pair of cards (before you separate them into two piles) you repeat one of the two phrases.

Also, make sure you don't show the face of the single card, either when your assistant is holding it, or as you're putting it on the selected pile. If they see the face of that card, they'll look for it in the second pile and it's not going to be there. The best way to be sure of this is to place each pair of cards between their knuckles so the cards face to the outside of the person's hand.

TWO CARD MEMORY

EFFECT: The top and bottom cards of the deck are shown to the audience and then put into the center of the deck. When asked the names of the new top and bottom cards, no one knows. You now show that the same two cards are still on the top and bottom of the pack.

PROPS NEEDED: A deck of cards

SECRET: As you have your audience memorize cards, one at a time, your fingers are working ahead of what you're actually saying.

ROUTINE: 1. Put the deck into your right hand to be held from above with your middle two fingers holding the outer end and your thumb holding the inner edge of the cards. As you apparently square the deck with your left hand, you actually bevel the bottom of the deck to your right.

2. Your left hand then takes the deck with your fingers at the top and your thumb on the bottom, pulls the deck away, turns it over, and puts it back face up in the right hand. As soon as your right fingers have a secure hold on the cards, your left middle finger slides the bottom card about a quarter of an inch to the right.

3. Remove your left hand and point to the deck. "I'm going to show you two cards."

PLAYING WITH CARDS

4. The left hand goes to the deck as the tip of your first finger pulls the second card out from the bottom about a half-inch and you ask for the name of that card.
5. You now point to the card on the face of the deck and ask for its name.

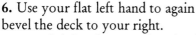

6. Use your flat left hand to again bevel the deck to your right.
7. Your left hand again takes the deck from your right hand, turns it over, puts it back, and your left middle finger again pushes the bottom card slightly to your right.
8. "The bottom card goes into the center of the pack."
9. Your left first finger goes to the deck, pulls out the second card from the bottom and puts it into the center of the pack without showing its face.

10. "And the top card goes into the center."
11. Your left thumb slides the top card off the deck and you slide it into the center of the pack.
12. "Now, do we know the names of the new top and bottom cards?"
13. If you've done everything smoothly, your audience should say no. "Ah, but we do."
14. Your left hand bevels the side of the deck and turns the beveled deck face-up so everyone can see that the same card is still on the face of the deck. Your left first finger pulls out the card on the bottom so everyone sees that it is still the same card on the top of the deck.

IMPORTANT POINTS: When you're removing the cards and putting them into the center of the pack, it should be done as casually as possible. You don't want to make a challenge of the action, but you want to give the impression that you merely want unknown cards on the top and bottom of the deck before going on.

ALL FOLLOW ME

EFFECT: A number of people are each given five cards and you also take five cards. They follow your moves by reversing several cards and not reversing others. At the finish, however, your cards are all face

HOUDINI'S SCHOOL OF MAGIC

down, but each of the other people has a card face up in the center of their packet.

PROPS NEEDED: A deck of cards

SECRET: Again, you do an extra move in such a way that it isn't seen by anyone because it looks very natural.

ROUTINE: 1. After each person has five cards, have the packets spread to make sure that all the cards are face down.

2. "Square up your cards," you tell your group, "and then take the top card and put it face up on the bottom." Holding the packet in the left hand Mechanic's Grip, take the top card of your packet, pull it toward you, turn it face-up, and put it on the bottom, but so that it sticks out about a half-inch past the outer end.

3. "Put the next card face down on the bottom." Your next card is pulled toward you, left facedown, and put on the bottom, but as you

square the packet this card is pulled toward you so its inner end is even with the inner ends of the rest of the cards in the packet.

4. "The next card is put face up on the bottom." Your third card is pulled toward you, turned face up, and put on the bottom, making it even with the other face up card that's sticking out.

5. "The fourth card is put on the bottom, still face down." Your fourth card is pulled toward you, left facedown, and put on the bottom, also even with the cards sticking out. As you square this card, your right thumb pushes slightly on the inner end of the top card to make sure that it is even with the third card down.

6. "Turn the top card face up and leave it on top." Now pull the top card and the third card together toward you, turn them face up as one card, and leave them on top.

7. "Turn your packet over and turn the top card facedown." You also turn your packet over and turn over the top card.

8. "So, if you did everything right, all your cards are still facedown." Of course, they're not because everyone except you has a card face up in the center of the packet. Naturally, they want to repeat the process and you can, but only one repeat is best.

IMPORTANT POINT: This is very good practice for keeping a packet of cards square because if you don't it's very obvious that your cards aren't really the same as everyone else's.

PLAYING WITH CARDS

IT TELLS ME. . .

This trick is to help you learn to cut a deck of cards so it stays neat while you're handling it. It's a very old trick, but still a good one.

EFFECT: Cutting a deck of shuffled cards into two piles, you look at the top card of one pile and say, "This card tells me that the top card of the other pile is the Four of Spades." You turn over the other card and it is the Four of Spades. You repeat this two more times, being correct each time. Then you name the top cards of both piles.

PROPS NEEDED: A deck of cards

SECRET: Cutting a deck of cards does NOT mix it up. All you do when you cut is change the top and bottom cards, the rest of the deck is still in the same order. Consider a deck as a complete circle with a slight break between the top and bottom cards. When you cut the deck you merely put that break at a different place in the circle; the order of the cards hasn't been changed. But, we don't let people who don't do card tricks know this as we can use it to our advantage.

PREPARATION: You have to secretly know the top card of the pack. As you shuffle the deck this shouldn't be hard to do, and let's say that it's the Seven of Spades.

ROUTINE: 1. Place the pack on the table face down, and cut it into two piles, with the top half being placed on the table farther from you than the bottom half.

2. Tell your audience what you're going to do, peek at the top card of the packet closer to you (the bottom half of the deck), remember 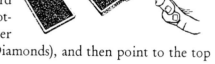 that card (say it's the Five of Diamonds), and then point to the top card of the other packet.

3. "That's the Seven of Spades," you say, and you turn it face up and drop it on the table.

4. Pick up the packet near you, drop it on the other half, and put the Seven of Spades face down on the bottom of the pack.

5. Cut the deck again into two packets, putting the top half on the other side of the bottom half, and  repeat the trick by remembering the card that you just peeked at and

97

naming the Five of Diamonds as being on the other packet.

6. Finally, after repeating the trick once more, say that you're going to name both cards. Cut the deck as before, and let's say that the new top card of the pack is the Ace of Clubs.

7. You now point to the card on the BOTTOM half of the deck, and say, "This is the Ace of Clubs," and you pick it up and put it in your left hand with its face toward you.

8. As soon as you see what card you have in your hand, point to the top card of the other half (the real Ace of Clubs) and call it by the name of the card in your hand.

9. Pick up that card, put in your left hand on your side of the first card, and drop the two of them face down on the table. You then put the two halves of the deck back together while someone else picks up the two cards to see if you're correct.

IMPORTANT POINTS: Each time you reassemble the deck in the first part of the trick, make sure you put two halves of the deck together and then put the named card on the bottom of the deck. All this action tends to make the spectators forget which half of the deck is which.

At the end of the trick, name the card you know, and pick up the card from the bottom half of the deck, but don't take too long looking at it. If you can, learn to recognize the card out of the corner of your eye so people can see that you don't look right at the card.

"SEVEN CARDS DOWN"

EFFECT: You run through the deck to find a certain card. You then show the face of that card to someone and tell him or her that you're going to write something on the card. Holding the deck so no one can see, you write something and shuffle the pack. A card is selected, remembered, and returned to the deck, which is then cut a number of times. You run the faces of the cards in front of the person who selected the card and ask them to remove the card you wrote on. When they do, it says how far to count down in the deck. You count off the correct number of cards and the selected card is the last card dealt.

PROPS NEEDED: A deck of cards. A pen that will write on playing cards

SECRET: It's all based on the fact that cutting the deck doesn't disturb the rotation of the cards.

ROUTINE: 1. Run through the cards to find a card that is fairly close

PLAYING WITH CARDS

to the bottom of the pack-that is a Two, Three, Four or Six (cards that have lots of white space on them. At the same time you count to see how far that card is from the bottom of the pack. Let's say that counting from the bottom of the pack, you find a Two of Hearts that's the seventh card from the bottom.

2. You turn all the cards below the Two at a right angle to rest of the deck, holding them with your left thumb, and show the faces to someone next to you. "I'm going to write something on the Two of Hearts," you say as you point to the Two.

3. Turning the deck so only you can see the faces, you now write "SEVEN CARDS DOWN". Naturally, if the Two had only been five cards from the bottom, you'd write "FIVE CARDS DOWN".

4. You now square up the cards and idly shuffle only the top half of the pack so that the bottom cards remain undisturbed. You do this with a simple overhand shuffle.

5. Run the cards face down from hand to hand so someone can select one, and while they're looking at its face to remember it, casually cut the deck in half.

6. Have the selected card returned to the top of the top half of the deck, and drop the bottom half on top of it. Now cut the deck twice, completing the cut each time.

7. Hold the deck up with the faces toward the person who selected the card and say, "I want you to remove the card I wrote on, the Two of Hearts." Now run through the pack so they can see the faces.

Wherever they find the Two of Hearts, cut the deck at that point as they remove the Two. Put the bottom half of the deck on top of the upper half and you're done. All they have to do is read the message out loud, you count that many cards down, and the selected card is at that number; in this example, the seventh card from the top.

THREE PILE SHUFFLE

This trick was selected to help you perfect the skill of dealing cards into piles and keeping them neat.

EFFECT: You make three piles of cards on the table, with the remainder of the deck staying in your hands. One card is dealt face up on top of each of the three piles and you show the next card to your audience so they can remember it. Gathering up the three piles and turning the face-up cards face down, you hand the deck to someone to shuffle. When you get it back, you deal the cards into a face-up pile, finally stopping on a card.

"That's the card you're remembering," you say, and you're correct. You now repeat the trick two or three times.

PROPS NEEDED: A deck of cards

SECRET: Somehow, you have to find out the name of the card that is fourth from the top of the deck. You can do this while shuffling or while gathering up the cards from a previous trick.

ROUTINE: 1. Hold the deck from above with your right fingers at one end and your thumb at the inner end and place the deck on the table a few inches to the left of center, but don't let go of the pack.

2. Cut off about a fourth of the deck from the bottom by riffling your right thumb up the inner end of the pack, lifting off the deck at that point. Repeat the process to make a second pile right in front of you and a third pile slightly to your right.

3. Put the remainder of the pack in dealing position in your left hand and deal off the top three cards one at a time, putting one face-up on top of each of the three piles.

4. While you turn your head away from the deck, pick up the next card from the deck and hold its face toward your audience so they can see it. "Remember this card," you tell them.

5. Drop the card facedown on top of the packet in your hand then gather up the three piles in any order, turning over the face-up cards as you do so, and put them on top of the other cards. Hand the deck to someone and ask him or her to shuffle it.

6. When the deck is returned to you, deal the cards into a face-up pile one at a time on the table, looking for the card that you remembered. Also, as you deal, remember the new fourth card from the top will be the card you show your audience when you repeat the trick. Now, keep

PLAYING WITH CARDS

dealing until you have dealt off the card that you first remembered.
7. Stop, point to the card, and name it as the card they are remembering.
8. Gather up the face-up cards, drop them on the packet in your hand, square them up, and you're ready to repeat the trick.

IMPORTANT POINT: As you reassemble the deck after showing the one card for them to remember, you can vary the procedure to throw off the thinking of your audience. The first time, pick up one of the face-up cards, turn it facedown on top of the remembered card, and then put that pile on top. Another time put a pile on the packet in your hand and then turn over the face-up card. You can keep varying the way you handle the cards, as it doesn't make any difference because you already know what the card is!

MAKE THEM MATCH
(Bill Coomer)

EFFECT: You run through the deck, remove a card, and put it face down on the table as a prediction. Dealing cards off onto the table into a pile you ask for someone to say stop. When they say stop, you put the remainder of the deck facedown on the table next to the smaller pile. The top card of the large pile is turned face-up and it's a Seven. You count off seven cards from the smaller pile facedown, and put the remainder of the packet to one side. When you turn the top card of the seven cards face-up, it's a second Seven. Turning over the top card of the small packet, it's a Seven, and when you turn your prediction card over it's the fourth Seven.

PROPS NEEDED: A deck of cards

PREPARATION: The deck is set up before you start the trick. Find two of the Sevens and put them on the face of the deck. Now put six cards below the two Sevens; that is, the two Sevens are now seventh and eighth from the bottom of the pack. Put another Seven on top of the pack, make sure that the fourth Seven is in the center of the deck and you're ready to go to work.

ROUTINE: 1. Remove the deck from its case, turn it so the faces are toward you, and run through the pack to find the fourth Seven, the one in the center of the deck. When you find it, put it facedown

101

on the table and tell everyone that it is a prediction.

2. Square up the deck, turn it face-up in your left hand, and start dealing cards face up onto the table. As you deal, you say, "I'm going to deal cards onto the table, and I want someone to just say the word 'Stop'."

3. When someone stops you, put the remainder of the deck facedown to the left of the face-up pile and turn the small packet facedown.

4. "Look," you say as you tap the top of the large pile. "You stopped me here. Let's see which card it is."

5. Turn the top card of the larger pile (the one on the left) face-up to show it is a Seven and leave it on top of the pile.

6. "That means that we have to count down seven cards," you say as you pick up the small pile. You count off seven cards facedown into a pile and put the remainder of that packet between the facedown pile and the one with the face-up Seven.

7. You turn over the top card of the seven cards you dealt off and it's a second Seven.

8. You turn over the top card of the middle pile and it's the third Seven.

9. You turn over your prediction and it's the last Seven. "I had a hunch that you'd find the lucky Sevens!"

IMPORTANT POINTS: Naturally, you can use any of the number cards rather than Sevens, but seven is a good average number for counting as it's neither too short nor too long. Just make sure that when you're setting up the deck that the cards you add below the two on the bottom of the pack equal one less than the value of the cards you're using. That is, if you were using Eights, then you'd put seven cards on the bottom.

When you're dealing cards to make that second pile and you're waiting for someone to tell you to stop, make sure you get past your two Sevens before you stop. If you deal the first card before you start telling them what you want them to do, then by the time you finish telling them you'll be get past the pair of cards you're about to force on your audience.

RIFFLE IMPOSSIBILITY

EFFECT: A spectator removes a card from the deck, remembers it, and returns it. The deck is shuffled twice then spread face-up on the table. Placing your hand lightly around the wrist of the person who selected the card, you move their hand back and forth over the face-up cards. Finally you stop, drop their finger on a card and say, "That's your card!"

PROPS NEEDED: A deck of cards in its case

SECRET: Beforehand you've placed all the cards of one suit, the Clubs for example, in proper rotation from Ace to King on the top of the deck with the Ace as the top card. Put nineteen other cards on top of them, put the deck in its case, put the case in your pocket, and you're ready for your first trick.

ROUTINE: 1. Take the case from your pocket, remove the deck from the case and spread the deck face down between your two hands so your helper takes a card from the thirteen cards in the center, the Clubs.

2. While they're looking at the card to remember it, spread the deck face down across the table, and tell them to return their card anywhere.

3. When they've done that, pick up the deck and riffle shuffle it twice.

4. Now spread the deck face up across the table so everyone can see all of the cards.

5. Take one wrist of the person who selected the card, have them stick out their first finger, and start running their hand back and forth along the face-up cards so the tip of their finger is about six inches above the faces of the cards. As you're telling everyone what you're about to do, find the Ace of Clubs.

6. Start looking to the right of the Ace to find the Two then look for the Three. Keep looking on through the Clubs until you find one that is out of order. Now look for that particular Club in the rest of the cards and when you find it, drop your helper's finger on that card. It will be the selected card.

IMPORTANT POINTS: If you want to see exactly how this trick works, go through the routine with the deck face up. You'll see that when you shuffle the first time that you may put a few cards between the Clubs but most of them will remain together and that the second shuffle will merely put a few more indifferent cards between them. The Clubs will stay in the same order, Ace to King, unless you have taken one out and put it elsewhere in the pack.

When you're looking through the spread-out Clubs, it's safest to search all the way through from Ace to King; just to make sure that only one card is out of place. Later, when you've learned to do better shuffles, it will undoubtedly be the first one out of order as you'll be shuffling so smoothly that you'll have almost the same number of cards between each Club.

SLOW-MOTION CROOKED STRAIGHT
(Lin Searles)

EFFECT: You are apparently able to deal cards from the center of the deck at will, as you continue to complete a Straight in an exhibition round of Poker.

PROPS NEEDED: A deck of cards

SECRET: Secretly place the Seven of Diamonds so it is the seventh card from the top of the deck and put the Eight of Hearts right below it.

ROUTINE: 1. Run through the cards, remove the following cards, and drop them face down on the table in front of you: any black Four, a red Five, a black Six, then the Seven of Hearts, and finally the Eight of Diamonds. Square up the deck in your left hand for dealing and turn the hand of five cards face-up in front of you.

2. "I have here a good hand to hold in the game of poker, a Straight, and I want to demonstrate how it's possible to get the cards you want regardless of where they are in the deck."

3. Turn the hand face down on the table. Next, take off the top card of the packet and put it on top of the deck. Take the next card and also put it on top of the deck.

4. "The two cards I need for my Straight are on the top of the deck, but I still have to deal the draw cards to the other players. Here's how to do that."

5. Quickly deal eight cards facedown into a pile and then deal the next two cards facedown on top of the poker hand.

6. Drop the facedown packet of cards back on the deck, then turn over and spread the poker hand to show that you still have a Straight. Turn the hand facedown again.

7. "Actually, the dealing wouldn't be done like that as I'd have to deal the cards as the players ask for them."

Put the top card of the hand back on top of the deck and put the next card on the deck as well.

8. "Let's say that the first player has Two Pair, so he only needs one card." Deal one card face down on the table.

9. "The next player isn't doing so well, so he wants four new cards."

Deal four cards as a group and drop the packet facedown on top of the single card on the table.

10. "The next player, an average player, has an average hand and only asks for three cards." Take off three cards and drop them on the facedown packet.

11. Without saying a word, deal off the next two cards, one at a time, and drop them on your poker hand. Reach over and spread it face-up on the table to show that it's still a Straight.

12. Drop the facedown packet of cards back on top of the deck and turn your hand face down.

13. "Doing that was easy because I knew that the cards I wanted were on top of the deck. Let's say that they're mixed in with the rest of the deck." Take the top card of the hand and put it near the bottom of the deck. Then take the next card and put it near the center of the deck. Do an overhand shuffle, keeping the top half of the deck in place, and get ready to deal.

14. "Let's go back to the beginning of the game where I have to deal out the original hands again." Separate the three facedown cards on the table and then deal three cards on top of each one.

15. Pick up the packets in any order, drop them on top of the deck, and deal out four poker hands. When you turn over your hand-it's the Straight!

IMPORTANT POINTS: The key to this trick is that you keep exchanging two pairs of cards that look alike (the Seven of Hearts and Eight of Diamonds with the Seven of Diamonds and Eight of Hearts), so never call attention to the suits of the cards in the poker hand. All the attention is directed to the fact that you have a Four to Eight Straight. Also, never say that you're dealing the second card from the top or dealing from the center of the deck. Let your audience draw its own conclusions, even though they're wrong.

EASY DOES IT
(Al Leech)

EFFECT: A card is selected and returned to the deck, but you fail to find it. You have a second card selected and returned to the deck, but as you deal off cards from the deck you manage to find the first card. You now spell the name of the first card, dealing off one card for each letter of the name, and the second selected card turns up on the last letter.

PROPS NEEDED: A deck of cards

SECRET: As you shuffle the deck, remember the bottom card, as this will be your key card.

ROUTINE: 1. Spread the deck between your hands so a card can be selected, and while it's being memorized, undercut the deck. That is, after the deck is squared, with your right hand pull the bottom half of the deck away from the left hand.

2. Have the selected card returned to the top of the packet in your left hand (the original top of the pack) and then drop the right-hand half on top of it. Your key card is now on top of the selected card.

3. Cut the cards so the two cards are near the top and then overhand shuffle the lower part, leaving the top intact.

4. Start dealing the cards, one at a time, face-up on the table as you look for your key card. The next card after your key is the selected card and you keep dealing. As you deal you spell the name of the selected card, dealing one card for each letter and starting with the selected card itself.

5. When you've dealt the last letter of the name, stop, and look at the person who selected the card. "Have I passed your card? I did? I thought I'd have some trouble. Well, I know that it's in this half, anyway."

6. Turn the face-up packet face down and leave it on the table.

7. Spread the rest of the cards that are in your hand so a second card can be taken. While it's being looked at, drop the cards in your hand on top of the packet on the table.

8. Pick up the deck, undercut it, and have the card returned onto the top half of the pack. Drop the cards in your right hand on top of it and cut the deck a few times.

9. Run through the cards with the faces toward you to find the first selected card. Cut the deck so that card is now the top card of the pack and put the deck face down in your left hand.

10. "I've found your first card at last. Name it."

11. They name the card and you deal the top card face-up onto the table.

12. "Now for your second card. Watch..."

13. You spell the name of the first card, dealing one card facedown on the table for each letter, and turn over the selected card on the last letter.

SPELLING MISTAKE

EFFECT: A card is selected, remembered, and returned. After running through the cards, you announce that you've found it. Spelling

the name of a card by dealing one card for each letter of the name, you turn up the card after the last letter. It's the card you spelled,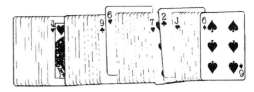
but it's not the selected card. You now spell the name of the correct card and it turns up after the last letter.

PROPS NEEDED: A deck of cards

SECRET: Use either the top card or the bottom card of the deck as your key card.

ROUTINE: 1. Have a card selected from the center of the pack, undercut the deck while it's being looked at, and have it returned to the top half, dropping the bottom half on top of it. Cut the deck a few times.

2. Run through the deck from the face of the cards up towards the top of the deck to find your key card. When you find it, the selected card will be either above it (if you used the top card as a key) or below it (if you used a bottom card key).

3. Keep running toward the top of the deck, but spell the name of the selected card, one card for each letter, and starting with the selected card.

4. When you've finished spelling the name of the card, look at the next card and spell the name of that card, continuing toward the top of the deck. If you get to the top of the deck and haven't finished spelling, just move to the bottom card and continue on.

5. When you've finished spelling the second card, cut the deck at that point, and hold the deck in dealing position.

6. "Well, I've found your card. Look, I'll spell it for you."

7. You spell the name of the second card, the one that wasn't selected by the spectator. On the last letter, turn over the card and look triumphant. Your audience will be quick to tell you that it's the wrong card.

8. "What card DID you take?"

9. As soon as they tell you, say, "Well, that's different." Quickly spell the name of the selected card and turn it over on the last letter. "See, it always works. You just have to have the right card!"

IMPORTANT POINTS: This is a good trick to do for people who have seen "Easy Does It," but not during the same session of card tricks. Do it at a later time.

PARACHUTE CARD

EFFECT: A card is selected and returned to the deck. The spectator names the card, the deck is dropped on the table, and the selected card flips face-up.

PROPS NEEDED: A deck of cards

SECRET: As you shuffle the deck, learn the name of the bottom card then overhand shuffle it to the top of the pack. You're ready.

ROUTINE: 1. Have a card removed and looked at while you undercut the deck. The card is returned to the top of the pack and the bottom half is dropped onto it.

2. Overhand shuffle the lower part of the deck and then cut it a few times. Run through the deck to find your key card, and the card right above it is the selected card. Cut the deck so this card is the top card of the pack.

3. Hold the deck in dealing position, but with your right hand over the top of the deck with your four fingers on the outside end and your thumb on the inner end. As you ask the spectator for the name of his card, your left thumb slides the top card about a half an inch to the right. Your right fingers should be positioned so no one can see that the top card is now jogged to the side.

4. Take your left hand away, and hold the deck about a foot above the table. Toss the deck straight down onto the table so the air currents can catch the outer edge of the top card and turn it face-up.

IMPORTANT POINTS: If you have trouble with the top card not turning over, try this. After you've slipped the top card to the right on top of the pack, lift the inner end a little and hold that break open with the ball of your right thumb. This will let air get in between the card and the rest of the deck a little more easily.

POCKET CHALLENGE
(Leo Behnke)

EFFECT: A spectator thinks of a number from 1 to 20 and counts that many cards off and puts them into his pocket. Using the same number, he again counts down into the deck, but this time he remembers the card that lies at that number. He now reaches into his pocket, removes some of the cards that are there, and drops them back onto the deck. The deck is cut a few times and given to you.

You look partway through the deck then close it up and look at your helper.

"I've not only found your card, but I've put it right back where it was when we started the trick. What was the number you thought of?"

You count off that many cards and when the spectator names the card he looked at, you turn over the next card. It's the selected card.

"Now may I have the nine cards still in your pocket, please? I like to keep my deck complete."

SECRET: For this trick you need two key cards. Remember the card that is the twenty-sixth card from the top (your "26 key") and the bottom card of the deck (the "bottom key"). Also make sure that you're working with a complete deck of fifty-two cards.

ROUTINE: 1. Idly overhand shuffle the top third of the deck while you ask someone to think of a number from one to twenty.

2. Now hand him the pack and tell him to hold it under the table so you can't see any of the action he's about to perform. Have him quietly count off the same number of cards 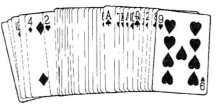 as the number he's thinking of and put those cards into a pocket.

3. Next, he's to count to that number again, but this time he's just to look at the card that lies at that number in the deck.

4. Finally, have him reach into his pocket, remove only some of the cards that are there, and drop them on top of the pack. He cuts the cards a few times and gives them back to you.

5. You run through the faces of the cards, starting at the bottom, until you find your 26 key.

6. Starting with your key, count off twenty-six cards toward the top of the deck and cut the deck at that point. Hold the deck in dealing position and look at the spectator.

7. "I've not only found your card, but

I've put it right back where it was when we started the trick. What was the number you thought of?"

8. When he gives you the number, start dealing cards, face-up and one at a time from left to right in a line across the table, and counting the cards out loud. As you count them off, watch for your bottom key and remember the number it falls on.

9. When you've dealt out his number, ask for the name of his card. Turn the top card of the deck face up on the table and it will be his card.

10. The number that you're remembering for your bottom key is the number of cards still in his pocket. Ask for that many cards back and have him count them out loud onto the table.

IMPORTANT POINTS: It's important that the spectator hold the cards out of sight while he works with them and does everything so quietly that you can't possibly have any clue as to what his number is.

When he has named his number near the end and you are dealing cards face up on the table, it helps if you jog your bottom key slightly out of line while you remember its number. Then, if you forget that number, you can mentally count to that card from the left end of the row of cards.

"26"

(Frederick M. Shields and Bascom Jones, Jr.)

EFFECT: Handing the deck to a spectator, you have him cut it into three facedown piles. He selects a card from the center of one pile, keeps it a secret, and you select a card from another pile, showing your card to everyone. The pack is put back together, cut a few times, and divided into two halves. You each take one half of the pack and every time you deal a card face-up onto the table, he deals one facedown from his packet. When you finally turn your selected card face-up, you have him turn over the corresponding card of his packet and there is his selected card.

PROPS NEEDED: A deck of cards

SECRET: This trick also depends on you remembering the 26th card from the top of the deck as your key card. Again, make sure that you have a deck that is complete with all fifty-two cards.

ROUTINE: 1. Hand the deck to someone and have them cut it into three facedown piles. As they do so, remember which pile is the top of the deck and which one is the bottom of the pack.

2. The card he selects must come from the bottom portion and be put on top of the top portion, but you make it look as though what happens is because of his choices. "Point to one of the three piles." Depending on which pile he points to, he does the following:
TOP: "Shuffle it and point to another pile."
CENTER: "I'll select a card."
Spread the packet face-up and point to your 26 key. "I'll use the (name)."
BOTTOM: "Shuffle it, remove a card, remember that card, and put it on top of the pile on the other end."
3. Regardless of what order he points to each of the three piles, those are the actions he goes through. So, now you each have a selected card, but everyone knows the name of your card.
4. Have him put the bottom packet on top of his card that's on the top packet, put the middle packet on top of those two, and cut the deck a few times.
5. Take the deck and hold it in dealing position. "We each need one half of the deck, so watch the cards as I deal them face-up."
6. Deal off twenty-six cards, one at a time, face-up on the table.
7. "Did you see your card in there?"
8. If his card is in the face-up pile, you turn the pile face down and give it to him. If his card is not in that pile, give him the packet still in your left hand and you take the tabled packet.
9. "I'm going to deal cards, one at a time, from the top of my packet and I want you to deal cards off your packet, card for card, right along with me, but deal yours facedown."
10. Start dealing your cards face-up and stop when you've just dealt your 26 key.
11. "There's my card, what's the name of the card you looked at?"
12. When he names it, have him turn over the last card he dealt and it will be his.
IMPORTANT POINTS: Remember, regardless of which pile he points to, something is done with it, but you have to give him the correct moves with each pile. His card comes from the bottom packet and is put on top of the top packet, and then the middle packet with your key card is put on top of them after you show your selected card.

HOUDINI'S SCHOOL OF MAGIC

TRICK FOR A BEAUTIFUL LADY

EFFECT: Three red Aces are shown, one at a time, with the remark that three Aces are had to beat in any game. But, you tell them, there is one card that's better. You have a woman name a number from one to three and when you count to that card and turn it over, it's now the Queen of Hearts.

"A beautiful woman can always find the Queen of Hearts!"

PROPS NEEDED: Three cards: Ace of Hearts, Ace of Diamonds, Queen of Hearts

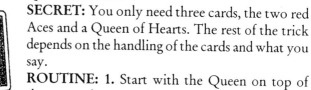

SECRET: You only need three cards, the two red Aces and a Queen of Hearts. The rest of the trick depends on the handling of the cards and what you say.

ROUTINE: 1. Start with the Queen on top of the two red Aces and all three cards facedown in your left hand in the Mechanic's Grip. You're apparently going to show all three cards, but you're going to keep the Queen hidden.

2. Push off the top two cards as one card, take the right edges with your right thumb and finger, and turn the two cards face-up on top of the third card. Again push off the top two cards, this time turning them facedown on top of the third card. Now push off just one card and put it under the packet.

3. Push off the top card, turn it over to show its face, turn it back facedown, deal it off, and put it underneath.

4. Push off the top card by itself, turn it over to show it, turn it back facedown, then deal it off and put it underneath.

5. Now make your remark about there being one card that is better than three Aces and have a woman name a number from one to three.

6. You now produce the Queen at that number by using one of the following moves. If she chooses-

One: You turn over the top card, the Queen of Hearts.

Two: Push off two cards as one, and put them under the packet. Again push off two cards, and turn them face-up to show the Queen. Then turn them facedown and drop the packet on top of the deck.

Three: Push off the top two cards as one and put them on the bottom, counting "One." Push off the next card by itself and put it underneath, counting "Two." Push off the next card and turn it face-up to show the Queen as you count "Three."

PLAYING WITH CARDS

IMPORTANT POINTS: When you push cards off the packet, regardless of whether it's one card or two cards, do it this way: Push the tip of your thumb down against the knuckle of your first finger, and then slide it to the right. If you want only one card, the tips of your left fingers will only let the top card slide. If, however, you want two cards to move, relax the tips of your fingers and two cards will move to the right and leave the third card where it is. Also, every time you turn cards face-up in your left hand, automatically square them up so only the face of the uppermost card shows.

SWITCH AND MATCH
(Paul Curry and David Altman)

EFFECT: You remove the Ace through Ten of Hearts and the Ace through Ten of Clubs from the deck. After arranging the Clubs in a certain order, you place them facedown on the table.

"That is a prediction of what you are about to do."

Taking the Hearts, you deal off cards, one at a time, and any time the spectator wishes, you switch the card you're about to deal for another one. After all ten cards have been dealt, you turn them over to show their mixed order. Then, turning over your prediction pile, you show that it is in the exact same order.

PROPS NEEDED: A deck of cards

SECRET: This trick involves a very subtle principle that is very difficult to see and understand without an explanation.

ROUTINE: 1. Remove the Ace through Ten of both the Clubs and Hearts.

2. Holding the Clubs so only you can see the faces, arrange them from top to bottom so they are in the correct order of Ace to Ten.

3. Now move the Ace, the Four, and the Seven, just one card to the right. The packet will now read: 2, Ace, 3, 5, 4, 6, 8, 7, 9, and 10. Hold the packet face down in your left hand.

4. "I have ten cards, the Ace through Ten of Clubs." Deal off the cards, face down and counting them one at a time, into a neat pile on the table. "These are my prediction cards."

113

5. Picking up the Hearts set them in order from Ace to Ten, from top to bottom.

6. Holding the packet facedown in your left hand, push the Ace into your right hand, push the Two off on top of it, turn them face-up, and drop them on the table. "That's what happens when we switch cards," you explain.

7. Push off the next card, turn it face-up, and drop the Three face-up on the other two cards. "That's what happens when we keep the cards the same."

8. So, if I switch cards," you say as you put the next card under the following one, remove the two, and drop them face-up on the pile, "you can see that the order of the cards is changed very dramatically."

9. Push off the next card as you repeat, "Nothing happens if I keep a card the same," and you drop the Six face-up.

10. "But every time I switch cards," you exchange the next two cards and drop them on the packet, "then the cards are changed."

11. Deal the last two cards, the Nine and Ten, one at a time onto the face-up pile, and spread the packet to show the faces. "As you can see, the cards get quite mixed up."

12. Pick up the pile and turn it facedown in your left hand, ready for dealing.

13. "Every time I start to deal a card, I want you to tell me whether I should keep it the same, or switch it."

14. Accordingly, you deal off single cards facedown onto the table if the spectator says, "Keep" and you switch the top two cards and drop them onto the packet when the person says "Switch."

15. After you've dealt the last card facedown, pick up the pile and deal the cards face up in a line across the table.

16. "Now let's look at my prediction cards."

Pick up your prediction stack, deal those cards face-up one at a time, from left to right, and each card above one of the cards already face-up. The two rows match, card for card.

THREE CARD MONKEY BUSINESS

(Bill Elliott, courtesy of Ibidem Magazine *and Pat Lyons)*

EFFECT: You tell a story about how you were victimized, long before you knew anything about playing cards, by a card sharper at a

PLAYING WITH CARDS

county fair. Having only three cards, you show them to be all red cards. Then, as your story explains, you start losing money because the cards become black ones when they shouldn't be. Finally, according to your story, you lose all your money because the final card is neither red nor black.

PROPS NEEDED: The Ace of Hearts The Ace of Clubs A Joker that has been colored with a green marker

SECRET: Arrange the three cards so the Joker is on top of the packet and the red Ace is on the bottom.

ROUTINE: 1. "I remember, when I was young and foolish, a time that I learned a lesson in how the world really works. This carnival sharper at a county fair showed me three cards, one at a time, and two of them were red and one was black."

2. Hold the packet facedown in your left hand with your right hand holding the ends of the cards from above between the tips of your right fingers and your thumb. Your right hand takes the packet and you turn it over to show the bottom card is red, "Red."

3. Turn the packet back down into the left hand.

4. Your left thumb pulls the top card into the left palm and your right hand turns over again to show the bottom card as being red, "Red."

5. Turn the packet back down so your left thumb can push the top card of the two to the right as the tips of your left fingers pull the bottom card of the two to the left and down onto the card on the left palm.

6. Turn your right hand over to show its card as black, "and black." Drop the card facedown on the other two.

7. "The black one was the one I was supposed to keep my eye on, but then he moved them around."

Spread the cards a little to the right and move the bottom card to rest between the other two, then square up the packet.

8. "He bet me a dollar that I couldn't find the black card. Now I knew he wanted me to say that it was the top one, but I outsmarted him. I said it was the bottom one. You owe me a dollar, he said."

Turn your right hand over to show the bottom card is red and turn it back down again.

9. "That was a slip of the lip, I said, I meant to say top. You want the top card? That's two dollars you owe me."

You now do what is known as the "Marlo Three-Way Alignment Move". With your right first finger, slide the top card toward you about an inch. Move the tip of your middle finger up to touch the back of the second card at the same time your thumb touches the back of the top card. Move the second card away from you, with your thumb pushing the end of the top card at the same time and you'll finish with the top and bottom cards aligned at the inner end. Use your first finger and thumb to pull the two cards toward you and turn them face-up as one card, but put just the tip of your left little finger under the right edge of the two cards so they rest on it and not on the third card.

10. After you've shown that the top card is apparently red, pull the two cards toward you (this is done easily because of the little finger break you obtained) and turn them facedown on top of the third card. "That's right, you win. I knew all the time that it was the middle card. The middle card, he says. That's three dollars you owe me."

11. Spread the cards a little, remove the middle card, turn it face-up, and put it between the other two in the spread. "Oh, I get it. You have four cards. No, he answered, only three, and he counted them."

12. Pull the cards one at a time into the right hand, so you reverse their order, turn the middle card facedown again, and square the packet in your left hand.

13. "Yeah, three cards, I said, but all three of them are red. If that's so, he says, then tell me where the red card is. Which red card, I asked. Any red card, he said. I couldn't lose, so I said it was the bottom one. Four dollars, is all he said."

14. Your right hand turns the packet over to show the bottom card is black, and keep the packet face-up. "I didn't mean the bottom card on that side, I said, I meant the bottom card on this side."

15. Point to the top card of the packet, which is now on the bottom of the face-up cards. "Five dollars was all he said."

16. Turn the packet facedown. Again use the Marlo Three-Way Alignment Move to show that the top card is black. Turn it facedown on top of the others in the left hand.

17. "Well, look, I said, if it isn't on the bottom and it isn't on the top, then it HAS to be in the middle. He looked at me and said that nothing HAS to be, and that I now owed him six dollars."

18. Spread the cards and turn the middle one over to show it as also

black, and keep it face up in the center.

19. "Look, he said to me in a low voice, you really shouldn't gamble as you only lose. I tell you what, if this card is black and this card is red (turn the bottom card face-up and leave it on the bottom), what color is this one? One dollar, I yelled. One dollar says that the top card is either red or black! You know, I never lost seven dollars so fast in my life."

20. You turn over the top card to show the green Joker.

IMPORTANT POINT: As you learn the moves try to always use the same moves to turn cards over. That way, when you have to do the Marlo move, it will look the same as the others.

HOUDINI'S SCHOOL OF MAGIC

PLAYING WITH CARDS SOME MORE

When you read the history of playing cards in the latest books about cards, primarily those by Sylvia Mann of England and Detlef Hoffmann of Germany, it seems that playing cards actually originated in three different continents. The earliest record is from India, and it seems that they were playing with their round cards there as far back as 1100 A.D. Shortly after that, in about 1120 A.D., there was a record written in China about playing card games with long, narrow strips of paper. The actual location for the third area is still up for grabs, but it was somewhere in the region of Egypt, Saudi Arabia, and Iran. Up until 1935 Iran was called Persia, so let's use that name for that entire area to make it easier.

The decks we use in the United States were developed from the decks used in Europe, and it seems that the European decks were based on the Persian decks, not only because of the design but also because of the timing. We don't know if the Italians or the Spanish were the first to have playing cards in their own country, especially since they both used the same suits, but it seems a very strong probability that they got them from the Persians. This could have been during the time that the Moors dominated all those countries from the eighth to fifteenth centuries, or through the biggest traders in the Mediterranean at that time, the Genoese and the Venetians. In any case, it seems that Spain and Italy got the cards, and liked them so much that they started making their own. The Persian cards were small rectangles, and the only changes the Europeans made were to make the cards a little larger and to alter one of the suits. The Persian cards used Coins, Cups, Swords, and Polo-Sticks as suits, but the Latins changed the sticks into Clubs; the Italians making only slight changes but the Spanish version becoming a tree limb used by Jack's giant.

In any case, the cards flowed from Italy and/or Spain up into Europe and, depending on each country, some other changes were made. Suits were changed, and sometimes the number of cards in the deck was also changed because of a certain game in each country. In a couple of hundred years, remember this is before the printing press came into being, almost every country had its own version of playing cards. A few packs even went with the sailors manning Columbus's ships, and it's said that the packs were thrown overboard when the sailors felt that the voyage was jinxed. Later, American Indians copied the decks used by the Spanish, and painted their versions on stiffened pieces of leather.

Today most of the decks are based on the same fifty-two card deck, with the usual Clubs, Hearts, Spades, and Diamonds, and are used to play a great variety of games and solitaire in almost every country of the world. It is now called the Standard deck, even though the numbers and the names of the court cards are called differently in each language. The leading manufacturers of cards in the world are the United States Playing Card Company in Cincinnati, the Hoyle Products company in St. Paul, the Austrian company of Ferd. Piatnik in Vienna, Carta Mundi based in Belgium, and Heraclio Fournier (partly owned by the U. S. Playing Card Co.) in Spain. These companies probably make three-fourths of the decks in the world, especially for countries that don't have their own card-making facilities.

SOME BASIC SLEIGHTS

We will now teach you some of the basic and simpler moves in sleight-of-hand with playing cards.

REVERSING A CARD

There are a number of different ways to secretly reverse a card in the deck, but we're going to teach you two easy methods.

VERSION 1: TOP OVER
1. To reverse the top card of the pack, hold the deck in dealing position and let your

arm drop to your side. With your thumb push the top card slightly to the right, catching the outer side of the card against your leg. Keep pushing on the card and turning the deck, pivoting the card on the edge against your leg, until your thumb is caught between the deck and the reversed card against your leg.

2. Slip your thumb out from between the card and deck and slide it between the reversed card and your leg, and then square the deck in your hand.

BOTTOM OVER

1. To reverse the bottom card of the deck, use your thumb to turn the deck over in your hand as you drop your arm to your side.

2. Go through the moves to reverse the card, and then twist the deck so it is again rightside up in your hand, that is, back again in dealing position.

3. When you bring the deck back up in front of you, it will be squared and no one can see the reversed card on the bottom.

VERSION 2: TWO-HANDED REVERSE

1. Hold the deck in dealing position in your left hand, but with your left thumb along the left edge and with your right hand over the deck, all four fingers on the outside end of the pack, and your right thumb on the inner end.

2. With the tip of your left little finger, pull down on the right corner of the bottom card until you can slip the tip of your finger between the card and the rest of the deck. Keeping your left thumb in place, pull down with your little finger until you can also get the tips of your second and ring fingers also on the top of the bottom card, keeping your first finger underneath.

3. Your fingers pull down on the card, using the left thumb as a hinge, until the card is at a right angle to the bottom of the deck, and then your middle

two fingers push on the back of the card to push it (reversed) up against the bottom of the pack.

At no time do you move your left thumb or your right fingers, and they serve as shields so no one can see what's happening on the bottom of the pack, and keep the top of the deck aimed toward your spectators' eyes to provide additional cover.

PALMING

VERSION 1: SWIPE PALM

1. Your left hand holds the deck at the tips of your left fingers, your first finger under the pack, the other fingers on one long side and with your thumb on the other side, your hand palm up, and the deck face down. Your right hand comes over the top of the pack with all four fingers together, and you place the pad of your right little finger on the outer right corner of the top card of the deck.

2. With your left hand pull the deck toward you with your right fingers pressing down against the top card, and tipping the deck upwards as you slide it backwards.

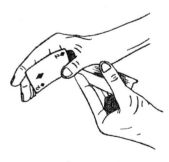

3. The deck will slide along the face of the top card, pushing it up into the palm of your hand, and the tip of your right little finger bends just enough to exert pressure between it and the base of your thumb. The first few times you may have to shift the card until you find the right position that holds the card securely and comfortably. This is the position you want for any time you palm a card, and your hand will learn to make any little adjustments as you do more and more palming.

VERSION 2: TIP-IN PALM

1. Holding the deck in the same position as the Swipe Palm, you talk to your audience while your right middle finger pushes the top card forward about an eighth of an inch.

2. At the proper time, depending on the trick and what you're saying, your right fingers move forward so the outer edge of the top card is in the crease of the first joint of your first finger. Your right fingers, held all together, now push down on the outer end of the top card and it will pop up into palming position.

VERSION 3: POP-UP COUNT

1. Hold the deck in the dealing position in your left hand and bring your right over the top of the pack so your right thumb is at the inner left corner of the deck and your first finger is curled lightly against the top card.
2. The ball of your right thumb now picks up the corners of however many cards you need to palm, and you slide the tip of your left little finger under those cards so you can shift the position of your right hand.
3. All of your right fingers are now held together and straightened out while your left ring finger joins your little finger under the top cards.
4. At the right moment, your two left fingers straighten out to pop the top cards up and into the palming position in your right hand.

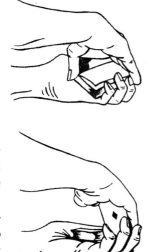

THE DOUBLE-LIFT

This move is very valuable in the arsenal of the card worker. It lets you turn over, show, and put back on the deck the top two cards rather than just the top card. In other words, you talk about the top card, but you actually use two cards.

VERSION 1:

1. Hold the deck in dealing position, bring your right hand over the top of the pack, and with the tip of your right thumb lift the inner left corner of the top two cards. Continue to lift the cards, turning them over so they're face up, and drop them back down onto the top of the deck.

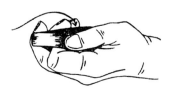

2. Name the card that's showing as the top card of the pack, and then pull down on the right side of the two cards so the left edge separates from the deck.
3. Again bring your right hand over the deck, pick up the inner left corner of the two cards, and turn them face down onto the deck.
If done smoothly and so that your audience doesn't see the left edges of the cards, you have a simple but powerful secret move.

VERSION 2:

1. Holding the deck in dealing position so your audience only sees the back of the top card, use your left thumb to riffle down the outer left corner of the deck to let the corners of the top two cards separate from the deck.

2. As your left thumb holds the break, bring your right hand over the deck, and put your middle finger on the outer corner and your thumb on the inner corner; lift the card (like turning the page of a book) until it's at a right angle to the top of the deck, and then slide that side of the two cards to the left so they're now face up.
3. To turn them face down your left fingers pull down on the right side of the two cards, and your right middle finger and thumb again take the left corners to turn them over. If you want, you don't have to let go of the two cards as soon as you turn them face up. Keep your middle finger and thumb in place as you turn them face up and then turn them face down again. It makes for a smooth turnover in what looks like one move.

DUPLICATION

PLAYING WITH CARDS SOME MORE

EFFECT: You look through the faces of the deck and remove one card which you put into your pocket without showing it. A spectator now names any number from one to twenty, and you count that many cards off onto the table. The card at that point is taken out, turned over, and left face up on the table. When you remove the card from your pocket and show it, it has the same value and suit. The trick can be repeated once more to show that it wasn't a coincidence.
PROPS NEEDED: Any deck of cards.
SECRET: The top part of the deck is arranged in matching pairs.
PREPARATION: Long before you do the trick, you look through the faces of the deck to find a card that matches the top card in color and value. For example, if the top card is the Four of Spades, then you look for the Four of Clubs and put it under the Four of Spades. If the next card is the Queen of Diamonds, then you look for the Queen of Hearts and put it under the first Queen. Keep doing this until you have eleven pairs (twenty-two cards) arranged on the top of the deck. Put the pack into its case and you're ready to dazzle your audience.
ROUTINE: 1. Remove the deck from its case, and idly overhand shuffle the bottom third of the deck as you explain that you need to put a certain card in your pocket as a prediction.
2. Hold the deck up and run through the bottom part of the deck and remove any card that isn't part of your setup. Without showing it to anyone, put it in your pocket. If you have a breast pocket in your shirt or jacket, put it there but so part of it still shows above the pocket.
3. Hold the deck face down in your left hand and ask someone for any number from one to twenty. When they give you a number you start dealing cards off the deck. Now the card you turn over for your assistant has to be one of the odd cards in the count; in other words, the first card of each matching pair in your setup.

So, if you're given an odd number, like thirteen, you deal that many cards face down into a pile, and give the last card dealt to your helper. If you're using an even number, like fourteen, you deal that many cards off into a pile, and then give the next card from the top of the deck to the spectator. Either way, this leaves the second card of that pair on top of the deck.
4. Tell the spectator to turn his card face up and leave it on the table,

and as he does this you secretly palm the top card of the deck.

5. Now you reach into the pocket that's holding your prediction card, but you push the palmed card to the tips of your fingers and pull it back out of your pocket.

If you're using your breast pocket, the tips of your fingers that are holding the palmed card go past the upper end of the pocketed card so your thumb can push the upper end of that card down into the pocket. You then push the palmed card out to your fingertips and remove it instead.

HERE OR HERE?
(Johnny Paul)

EFFECT: A card is selected from a shuffled deck, looked at, and returned. The deck is again shuffled, and then held in dealing position. The helper is asked to tell you when to stop as you deal through the cards. You deal cards off the top of the pack, one at a time, face down onto the table, until the spectator says to stop.

"What was the name of your card? Good, and do you think it's here," you say as you point to the small pile on the table, "or here?" as you hold up the deck.

Your helper gives his answer, but you tell him he's wrong, that it's here, and you lift your right hand from the table, turn over the card that has appeared underneath, and it's the selected card.

PROPS NEEDED: A deck of cards.

ROUTINE: 1. After someone has selected a card from the deck and is looking at it, spread the deck between your two hands so the card can be returned to the center of the pack.

2. As you close up the spread, push the tip of your left little finger up against the face of the card just above the selected one so there will be a slight separation between the two cards as you square the pack. Now push the fleshy part of the ball of your right thumb into that break at the inner end of the deck as you turn the deck to do an overhand shuffle.

3. Shuffle off most of the bottom of the pack into your left hand, then tip those cards onto your left thumb as you drop all of the cards in your right hand (up to the break) so they fall on top of the cards in your left, then tip all the cards in your left hand back to the right so you can drop the remainder of the pack from your right hand onto the bottom of the packet in your left. It should look as though you've

shuffled the pack with a cut at the end.
4. As you explain to your helper that you're going to deal off cards and that he should tell you to stop at any time, you palm off the top card of the deck in your right hand.
5. Put your right hand on the table a little to your right and lean on it, and then start dealing cards of the top of the deck using just your left hand. Push the cards off, one at a time, with your left thumb and let them drop face down onto the table into a pile.
6. When you're stopped, ask for the name of the selected card. Thenuse your left first finger to point to the pile on the table, "Do you think it's here...", you ask, and then you hold up the deck in your left hand, "or here?"
7. After they answer, you say, "Oh, no, that card is over here." You lift your right hand, pick up the card you palmed, and turn it over to show it as the selected card.

MIRASKILL
(Stewart James)

EFFECT: As someone shuffles the deck, you write a prediction on a piece of paper and put it face down on the table. You then instruct the spectator to take cards off the top of the deck, two at a time, and turn them face up. If both cards are red, they're to be dropped into one pile; if both cards are black, they're to be dropped into a second pile; and if the cards don't match in color, they're to be dropped into a third pile. When the entire deck has been dealt into the three piles, you have your prediction read out loud.

It says that there will be four more red cards than black cards, and when the red and the black piles are counted, the prediction is correct. You can then make a second prediction that is different, and it will also be correct.

PROPS NEEDED: A deck of playing cards, pencil or pen and a file card or small sheet of paper

SECRET: This trick depends on a mathematical principle called parity. Since a deck of cards has an even number of red cards and the same even number of black cards, if you remove any small even number of cards of either color, you will have that many more cards of the other color in its pile at the end of the dealing.

PREPARATION: Sometime before the trick is to begin, steal four black cards out of the deck and put them into a pocket that will be easy to get into while you're seated.

ROUTINE: 1. When you want to do the trick, give the deck to someone to shuffle while you write your prediction. Write, "You will have four more red cards than black ones," and turn the prediction face down on the table.

2. Now tell your helper how you want him to deal the cards into the three piles, and sit back to watch. As he is dealing, casually reach into your pocket, and palm out the four cards you've hidden there. Keep your hand in your lap.

3. When all the cards are on the table, push the prediction toward him with your empty hand and tell him to read it out loud. You then pick up the pile that has the mixed red and black cards in it, turn it over, and drop it near the edge of the table.

4. After the red pile and the black pile have been counted use your empty hand to pick up one of the piles and turn it over as your hand with the palmed cards goes on top of the facedown pile. The palmed cards are laid on top as you pull the pile to the edge of the table and pick it up. Reassemble all the piles into a neat deck.

5. As you have it shuffled again you can write a second prediction, but this one has to say, "You will have the same number of black cards as red ones." Again, you will be correct.

IMPORTANT POINT: However many cards of an even number and all of one color that you steal out of the deck, there will always be that many extra cards of the opposite color. If the deck is a complete pack of 52 cards, then the two piles of cards will always have an equal number of cards, and that number will depend on how many pairs of mixed colors were dealt into the third pile.

THE SPECTATOR FINDS IT

EFFECT: Any spectator shuffles and cuts the deck into two piles. Taking one of the two halves, he puts it behind his back, removes the top card and puts it onto the bottom of the packet, and then takes the new top card into his other hand. Bringing them back in front of him, he looks at the card, drops it on top of his packet, and you put the other half of the deck on top of it.

Your helper then puts the entire deck behind him, again puts the top card on the bottom. He takes the next card, turns it over, and puts it into the center of the deck.

PLAYING WITH CARDS SOME MORE

When you get the deck you riffle the ends of the cards to make the magic happen, and then spread the deck across the table. One card is face up. You turn over the card next to it, and it's the selected card.

PROPS NEEDED: A deck of playing cards

SECRET: You have to reverse two cards in the half of the deck that the spectator isn't using.

ROUTINE: 1. Ask someone to shuffle the deck and then cut it into two halves. When she takes the half she wants to work with, you take the other half.

2. Drop the arm holding the packet to your side, standing so your leg is hiding your hand, as you ask her to put her half behind her back. Tell her to put the top card on the bottom, as you secretly push off the top two cards of your packet and reverse them together, and then reverse just the top card. This means that the second card from the top is reversed and the top card is face down.

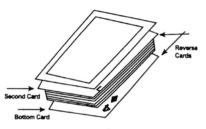

3. Now reverse the bottom card of your packet, and bring the packet up in front of you in normal dealing position. Meanwhile, your helper has taken off the new top card of her packet and brought them in front of her.

4. Have her look at her card and drop it on top of her packet. You reach over and drop your packet on top of hers. Tell her to put the deck behind her back again.

5. She removes the top card of the deck and puts it on the bottom of the pack. She takes the next card (the one that is secretly reversed), turns it over, and puts it into the center of the deck. Now she brings the deck out in front of her.

6. Riffle the end of the cards to apparently work the magic, and then spread the cards across the table. One card is face up, apparently the one she reversed. Remove the card just below the reversed one (the one toward the bottom of the pack), ask her to name the card she looked at, and turn the card over to show that it's hers.

REVERSE MISTAKE

EFFECT: A spectator removes a card from the deck, remembers it, and returns it to the deck. After announcing that you're going to reverse the selected card so quickly that no one will be able to see you do it, you riffle the end of the deck with your thumb. The deck is spread across the table to show that a card is reversed, but your helper says it's the wrong card. So, using the value of the reversed card, you count away from it and on the last number you turn over that card to show the selected card.

PROPS NEEDED: A deck of playing cards

PREPARATION: You can either have a card reversed in the deck before you start doing card tricks, so that this is the first trick of your routine, or you can reverse the needed card as you shuffle the deck.

Using the overhand shuffle, shuffle until you see a card with a value of six or less on the bottom of the packet, then drop the rest of the cards on top of the deck. Now you reverse that card you spotted, and then shuffle cards below it to equal one less than its value. If it was a Six, then you'd shuffle five cards to lie below it. Now you're ready to go into the routine.

ROUTINE: 1. Start running the cards from hand to hand, starting at the top of the deck, so that someone can remove any card, and make sure that you don't expose the reversed card near the bottom. As he looks at his card to remember it, close up the deck and cut it into two halves.

2. He returns his card to the top half and you drop the bottom half on top of it. Hold the deck in dealing position and with the right hand holding the ends of it. Tell your audience that you're going the reverse the selected card so fast that no one will see you do it.

3. Riffle the inner ends of the cards with your right thumb.

"Did you see me do it?" you ask.

4. "Well, I did it," you say, as you spread the deck face down across the table. "There it is!"

5. Your helper will immediately let you know that the reversed card is not his selection, so you pretend to think for a moment.

"All right," you say. "We'll use the value of that card to find your card. Look. . ."

6. Using the value of the reversed card, start counting with the next card toward the bottom of the pack, and pick up the card at the last number.

"What's the name of your card?"

Turn over the card in your fingers to show that you finally found the right one.

ELEVATOR CARDS
(Ed Marlo)

EFFECT: You show the Ace, Two, and Three of any suit, and deal them onto the table one at a time. The Three is then placed on the bottom of the deck, the pack is riffled, and the Three jumps to the top. The Two is placed on top, the pack riffled again, and the Two is now on the bottom. Finally, the Ace is put into the center of the deck, the cards are riffled, and the Ace is now on top of the deck.

PROPS NEEDED: A deck of cards

ROUTINE: 1. Run through the faces of the cards until you find the Three of any suit, say the Clubs. Remove it and place it on top of the pack. Now find the Two, remove it, and put it on top of the Three. Now find the Ace of Clubs, but push it even with the card just above it, take the two of them out and put them on top of the deck, handling them like one card.

2. Square up the pack and put it into your left hand in dealing position, and use the second method of making a Double-Lift to get a break under the top two cards.

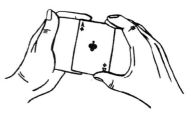

3. Pick up the top two cards with your right hand and turn them face up, handling them as one card. Shift your right fingers so you're now holding the two cards at the center of each end.

"The Ace," you say.

4. Your left thumb pushes the next card until it's over the right side of the deck for half its width, and use the 84
cards in your right hand to turn the Two face up, and then slide it onto the face of the Ace.

"The Two," you say.

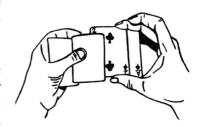

5. Again, push the top card of the deck to the right and turn it over with the cards in your right hand to show it as the Three, and put it on

HOUDINI'S SCHOOL OF MAGIC

top of the faceup Two in your right hand.

"The Three. Remember, the Ace, the Two, and the Three," you say as you turn all three cards over onto the top of the deck.

6. Deal three cards, one at a time, onto the table in a line from left to right in a facedown row. Actually, the cards are, from left to right: some unknown card, the Ace, and the Two.

7. Drop the deck onto the card at the right end of the row, pick them all up, and riffle the inner end of the deck from the bottom up toward the top. Turn over the top card and drop it face up on the table.

"The Three."

8. Pick up the middle card, put it on top of the deck, riffle the end of the deck downwards, and turn the deck over to show the Two. Deal it off onto the table.

"The Two."

9. Pick up the remaining facedown card and slide it into the center of the pack. Give a quick riffle to the deck, turn over the top card, and deal it onto the table as you say, "The Ace."

PROCESS OF ELIMINATION

EFFECT: After a card has been selected, memorized, and returned to the pack, you say that you don't have to go looking for the card because the deck will tell you what it is.

You show the bottom card to your helper and ask if that card is the same color as the selected card. You cut the deck and show a new bottom card and ask if this card is of the same suit. Apparently the answers are wrong because you have to ask for the name of the card. As soon as it's named you spread out the deck and the selected card is now face up in the center.

PROPS NEEDED: A deck of playing cards

SECRET: Even though this trick doesn't use a double-lift to pick up two cards, you use the same moves to accomplish the trick.

ROUTINE: 1. Spread the deck between your hands so someone can

take any card they want. When they return the card, after they look at it, you close up the deck, but keep the tip of your left little finger against the face of the card just above the selected one.
2. Transfer that break to the ball of your right thumb as your right hand holds the deck from above. Hold the deck square and cut it somewhere below the break, complete the cut, then cut at the break, and complete the cut. The selected card is now on top.
3. Shuffle just the bottom half of the deck so the selected card stays on top.
4. As you tell your audience that the deck will tell you which card was selected, your right thumb separates the inner end of the top card slightly from the rest of the deck. With your thumb holding that break, cut the deck in the center, turn the bottom half face up, and drop it on top of the selected card, but don't let go of the break.
5. Point to the faceup card and ask, "Is this card the same color as your card?"
If the question is correct, then you're ahead. If they tell you no, then say, "Then the process of elimination means that your card was (the opposite color)."
6. Again cut the deck, this time at the break, turn the bottom half face up, but hold it in your left hand. Point to the card on the face of that half with the first finger of your right hand, and ask, "Was your card the same as this suit?"
7. This time, regardless of whether they answer yes or no, you drop the right half onto the left half. Square the deck and act as if you have lost the selected card. Hold the end of the deck up to the level of your eyes, riffle the inner ends of the deck as if you're looking into the deck, and ask for the name of the card. Place the deck face down on the table.
8. "Oh, that one! That's the one I always keep face up in the deck in case I need it." You then spread the cards to show that the selected card really is face up in the center of the pack.

UP AND DOWN

EFFECT: You show ten cards, separate them into two packets, put the packets face to face, and have them shuffled together. You put the cards behind you and announce that you'll divide the pack into two equal halves and that there will be the same number of faceup cards in each half.

HOUDINI'S SCHOOL OF MAGIC

After successfully doing that, you even repeat it a couple of times, but no one else can do it.

PROPS NEEDED: Ten playing cards

ROUTINE 1. Separate the cards into two packets of five cards each.

2. Put the two groups face to face and shuffle them, making sure that no cards get turned over.

3. Give the packet to someone else to mix as well and then take them back.

4. With the packet behind your back, count off the top five cards, turn them over, and bring each group in front of you, one packet in your left hand and the other in your right. Show everyone that the same number of face up cards are in each half.

5. As you put the two packets together again, turn one of them over.

6. Shuffle the cards again, and put them behind your back.

7. Again take off the top five cards, turn them over, and bring out the two packets.

8. Just before you give the cards to someone else to try, put the two groups together but don't turn one packet over first. It will not be impossible for anyone to get the same number of faceup cards in each half.

MONEY MAGIC

When you can do tricks with money, you can do tricks absolutely anywhere. There will always be someone in your audience, large or small, who will have a coin or bill so you can create a little magic. Money is also a popular subject and your spectators will always be interested in what you are about to tell and show them.

CHANGE OF A PENCIL

EFFECT: To prove the power of money, you roll up a dollar bill and hold it between your thumb and first finger. Someone else holds the two ends of a pencil as you hit the center of the pencil with the rolled bill. Oddly enough, the pencil breaks into two pieces.
PROPS NEEDED: A full-length wooden pencil, a dollar bill
SECRET: You insert a finger into the action, unknown to your audience.
ROUTINE: 1. Roll up the dollar bill along its length so you finish with a tight paper tube six inches long. Bend your right hand into a fist and hold one end of the bill between the tip of your thumb and the joint of the first finger just below the knuckle, with the bill at a right angle to your closed fingers.

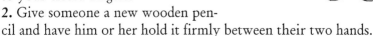

2. Give someone a new wooden pencil and have him or her hold it firmly between their two hands.
3. Hit the center of the pencil once or twice lightly with the bill, as though you're concentrating on exactly where you want to strike.

4. On the third stroke, extend your first finger alongside the bill and come down hard on the pencil. Immediately curl your finger back with the others so only the bill is showing. The pencil will be broken, but when others try it they'll fail because they're using just the bill.

IMPORTANT POINTS: To get into the trick, you can talk about karate and how concentration will increase the power of a simple blow, or you can talk about the power of money to overcome any obstacle.

QUICK VANISH

EFFECT: You wrap a coin in a handkerchief, but when you open it back up the coin is gone.

PROPS NEEDED: A handkerchief A piece of soft wax (or one of the soft plastic adhesives called Stick-Tak or Tac 'N' Stik)

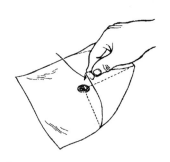

PREPARATION: You have prepared your handkerchief ahead of time by putting a small piece of sticky wax or soap near one corner of the hem. Fold the handkerchief so the wax is to the outside and put the hank in your pocket.

ROUTINE: 1. While you're asking for the loan of a penny or dime, remove the handkerchief from your pocket, open it out, and lay it on the table so the piece of wax is on top of the lower right corner. Stand with your hand over that corner so no one sees the wax.

2. Put the coin in the center of the handkerchief and fold the waxed corner over the coin, pressing the wax down onto it. Fold the other three corners in and past the center so they also cover the coin.

3. Put your two hands at the opening right in front of you and open it up by sliding your hands apart. The folded handkerchief will open up and the waxed coin will come into your right hand.

4. Shake the hank a couple of times as your right fingers pull the coin and wax away from the cloth, and hide it in your fingers. Toss the

MONEY MAGIC

handkerchief onto the table for examination as you casually pocket the coin.

IMPORTANT POINTS: By asking at your local stationery store, you'll find some temporary plastic adhesives like Tac'N Stik, Stick-Tak, or some other brand name. They work very well as your secret gimmick in the corner. As you fold the waxed corner up to the coin, start folding a second corner at the same time so not all of your audience's attention is on the first corner.

FIFTY TO ONE

EFFECT: Showing a penny and a half-dollar on your hand, you put the penny in your pocket and the half inside a handkerchief. Someone holds the handkerchief while you snap your fingers to make the two coins change places. The handkerchief is opened to show the penny and you remove the half-dollar from your pocket.

PROPS NEEDED: A penny, a half-dollar

SECRET: Again, some wax, soap, or plastic adhesive is used to make a minor miracle. Put a very small amount on a penny then stick it to a half-dollar near one edge.

ROUTINE: 1. Take the two coins from your pocket with your left hand as you ask for the loan of a handkerchief. If you can, have two or three loose coins in your hand with the two waxed coins.

2. Hold the money so the waxed penny is showing on top of the half-dollar. Put the loose coins back in your pocket, and call attention to a penny and a half-dollar.

3. Pretend to take the penny, but actually turn the two coins over behind your right fingers. Holding your right hand as though it has the penny, hold it up for a second as though you're showing it and put your hand in your pocket, apparently leaving it there.

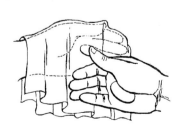

4. Your right fingers now take the half-dollar and, as you put it under the center of the handkerchief, you separate the two coins and leave the penny in the cloth.

5. Take your hand out from underneath with the half-dollar hidden

in your fingers and wad up the handkerchief.

6. Snap the fingers of your other hand, command the two coins to change places, and have someone open the handkerchief.

7. After the penny drops out, reach into your pocket and bring out the half-dollar at your fingertips.

IT'S THAT ONE

EFFECT: Three bottle caps, a quarter or nickel, and a pen are laid out on the table. After covering the coin with one of the caps, you turn your back while someone mixes them about. When you turn back you balance the pen across your fingers and move it along the line of caps. Suddenly the pen dips over one of the caps and when you pick it up, there is the coin.

PROPS NEEDED: Three bottle caps, a quarter or nickel, a hair about one inch long, some glue, a pen

PREPARATION: You have glued a quarter of an inch long hair to one side of the coin you're going to use. As a matter of being prepared, you should probably prepare two coins, one with a dark hair to use on wooden tables and one with a white or light hair to use on tablecloths. Put the two coins in separate pockets so you know which one to use as soon as you see the table.

ROUTINE: 1. Remove the bottle caps, the pen, and finally the coin. Lay the coin on the table with the hair on the bottom then turn your back.

2. Ask someone to cover the coin with one of the three caps and move them around so you won't know which one is hiding the coin. When they're done, you turn back around.

3. Lay the pen across your first two fingers so that it's very close to the balance point. Move your hand slowly over the row of caps until you spot which cap has the hair sticking out from under it. When the pen is over that cap, all you have to do is lift your ring finger slightly to make the pen move and point downwards at the selected cap.

COIN BOX

EFFECT: After showing an empty matchbox, you close it and set it to one side. You now drape a handkerchief over your left hand,

MONEY MAGIC

poke a small pocket down into it, and drop a quarter inside. You snap your fingers to make the magic happen, take one corner of the handkerchief, shake it out to show the coin is gone, and open the box to dump out the coin.

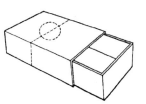

PROPS NEEDED: An empty matchbox, two duplicate coins, a handkerchief, a small rubber band

SECRET: You have two coins that look the same and have the same date.

PREPARATION: Open the drawer of the matchbox and wedge one coin between the inside of the cover and the top edge of one end of the drawer. Snap a small rubber band around the base of the middle two fingers of your left hand. A handkerchief is folded up and put into a pocket.

ROUTINE: 1. Show that the matchbox is empty and close it by holding your fingers at one end and your thumb on the end of the drawer. This way, the coin will drop into the drawer without anyone seeing it.

2. Bring out the duplicate coin and your handkerchief, putting the coin on the table and draping the handkerchief over your left hand.

3. While your right hand is picking up the coin, use your left thumb to open the rubber band and slip it up near the tips of your fingers.

4. Push a pocket into the hank so it goes down inside the rubber band and drop the coin into it.

5. Close your left fingers and let the rubber band slip off so it holds the coin inside the pocket.

6. Take one corner of the handkerchief, shake it out to show the coin is gone, and immediately have someone open the matchbox. As they're doing that, you can put the handkerchief back into your pocket.

HOUDINI'S SCHOOL OF MAGIC

SHRINKING QUARTER

EFFECT: You place a dime in the center of a playing card, draw a line around the coin, and fold the card in half so you can cut a hole the size of the dime. Flattening out the card, you challenge anyone to push a quarter through the hole. When everyone decides it's impossible, you stick a finger through the hole and push on the quarter.

You then tell them that it can also be done legitimately. Folding the card in half you put the coin inside the folded halves of the card until it comes to rest in the small hole. When you snap your fingers, the coin drops through the small hole and onto the table.

PROPS NEEDED: Two duplicate court cards with matching backs, a dime, a quarter, a pen or pencil, a pair of scissors or sharp knife, a razorblade

PREPARATION: Remove a face card from an old deck, put it on a  piece of cardboard, and with a razorblade, cut a 1 1/4" slit at one end. The slit has to be right along the outside of the line that forms the border of the card. Don't cut the slit in the center of the line, as it will show. Have a quarter, a dime, a sharp knife or heavy scissors, and a pencil handy when you start the trick.

From a deck with a matching back remove the duplicate of the card you've just gimmicked. Fold it in half, draw a dime-sized circle in the center, fold it in half, and cut out the circle. This second, ungimmicked card should be folded in half and put into a separate pocket.

ROUTINE: 1. Drop the gimmicked card on the table, followed by the dime, the pencil, and scissors.

2. Put the dime in the center of the face of the card, draw a line around it, and then fold the card in half so you can cut around the line to make a hole. However, when you fold the card you do it so the ends of the card don't match; that is, the corner of one end should be just slightly higher than the corner of the opposite end.

3. Cut a hole in the edge of the fold by following the line.

4. Open out the card and challenge anyone to push the quarter through the hole.

5. Regardless of whether the challenge isn't accepted or if someone else knows the joke of pushing the coin through the hole with a finger or the pen, you're set up for the actual trick.

MONEY MAGIC

6. Fold the card in half so the slit end is on your side of the card, pick up the quarter, and slide it between the two sides of the card, making sure that everyone sees that the coin does go inside the fold.

7. Bring the coin to the center of the end of the card and slide its bottom edge down through the slit. With your thumbs, slide the coin down until its lower edge is even with the two corners of the hole in the center. It now looks as though the coin is resting inside the fold and on the edges of the hole.

8. Remove one hand so only one thumb is holding the coin in place, snap your fingers, and release the coin so it drops onto the table.

9. Open up the card, give it a snap, and drop it in the pocket that holds the duplicate card.

10. Pick up the coin, flip it in the air, and put it in the same pocket. Now if someone wants to examine the props, you can remove the ungimmicked card and the coin and let them worry about them all they want.

IMPORTANT POINTS: The way you put away the card and coin at the end of the trick is important. It should happen with a 1-2-3 timing, like you're totally unconcerned. Then, when someone asks for the props, you can be very helpful and give them the wrong card. That's the way sneaky magicians do it.

A FIFTH POCKET

EFFECT: Explaining that you sometimes need a fifth pocket for your money, you put a coin against the cloth of your pants leg and pull a fold of cloth over it to form a small pocket. When you let the cloth open up again, the coin is gone. Reaching into your pocket you remove the same coin.

PROPS NEEDED: A quarter or half-dollar

SECRET: Again, you have to learn to do a secret move, but it's covered so well that you won't have any trouble with it. Just remember that everything should be relaxed and look very natural.

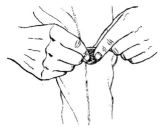

ROUTINE: 1. Place the coin on the outside of your right pants leg, about six inches above your knee and with the tips of both middle fingers holding the coin against your leg.
2. Pinch the cloth above and on each side of the coin then twist the coin downward to pull the cloth down over the coin so it's completely covered.
3. Slide your right fingers out of the pocket, secretly taking the coin with them, while your left first finger holds the cloth fold in place.

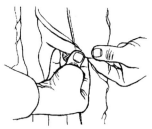

4. With your right fingers hiding the coin, place your right hand about four inches below the fold and pinch the cloth the cloth between your thumb and first finger. Your two hands pull in opposite directions to pull the fold open.
5. Wait one second so everyone can see that the coin is gone, brush off the cloth where the coin was, and reach into your pocket with your right hand to bring out the coin.

SLOW NICKEL VANISH

EFFECT: Holding a borrowed nickel in your left fingers, you spread a napkin or handkerchief over it. Your audience sees the shape of the coin right up to the last second, but when the cloth is pulled completely off your left fingers, the coin is gone.
PROPS NEEDED: A handkerchief or cloth napkin, a borrowed nickel
SECRET: Even though you do this trick at a very slow speed, it is very deceptive. Your right hand actually steals the coin and gets rid of it. You should be wearing a coat for this trick, although a shirt with a pocket will work if the cloth is thick enough to hide the coin.

ROUTINE: 1. Borrow a nickel and hold it at the tips of your left first finger and thumb with the other fingers closed. Hold a napkin in the center of one side in the right hand so most of the napkin drapes down. Spread your first finger and thumb as far apart as possible, letting the tips of your first finger and middle fingers hold the hem of the cloth, while the rest of your fingers hold their part of the napkin against the base of your thumb.

2. Hold the napkin below your left hand and bring the cloth up and over the tips of your left fingers. As your right hand comes over the coin, the tip of your right thumb steals the coin by gripping it against the side of your first finger.
3. Without slowing or stopping, keep moving the cloth over your left hand as your left thumb moves up to imitate the shape of the coin under the cloth. Adjust the distance between your left hand and your chest so that your right hand is over your breast pocket just as the center of the napkin is over your left fingers.

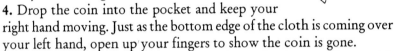

4. Drop the coin into the pocket and keep your right hand moving. Just as the bottom edge of the cloth is coming over your left hand, open up your fingers to show the coin is gone.
5. Drop the napkin on the table and apologize for the complete vanish of the coin. Offer to reimburse the owner sometime in the future.

TWENTY-FIVE CENTS

EFFECT: Two dimes and a nickel are arranged in a row on the table. The two dimes are dropped into your left hand and the nickel is put in your pocket. When your left hand is opened, however, there are the two dimes and the nickel. Again, two coins are put in the left and the third into your pocket, but all three are produced from the left hand. Finally, just the nickel is put into your hand and the two dimes put away. But when your hand opens this time you have a quarter.

PROPS NEEDED: Three dimes, Two nickels, a quarter

PREPARATION: Have two dimes and a nickel in your left pocket and the quarter and third dime in your right-hand pocket. The extra nickel is hidden in the fingers of your right hand.

ROUTINE 1. Remove the three coins from your left pocket and arrange them in a row in front of you as you say, "Look, twenty-five cents."
2. Pick up one of the dimes and drop onto the palm of your outstretched left hand.
3. Pick up the second dime and drop both it and the secret nickel into your left hand as your left fingers close over the coins.

4. Pick up the nickel from the table, show it, and put it in your pocket. Your fingers then bring the extra dime out of your pocket but keep it hidden.

5. Rap the knuckles of your left hand against the table then open it to drop all three coins on the table. "Twenty-five cents," you say.

6. Pick up one dime and drop it into your left hand, then drop the nickel and extra dime into your closing left hand.

7. Pick up the second dime, put it in your pocket, and exchange it for the quarter.

8. Rap your left knuckles again, open your hand, and drop out the three coins. "Twenty-five cents," you repeat.

9. Pick up the nickel, bring it to the left hand, but drop the quarter into the closing fingers, secretely retaining the nickel.

10. Pick up a dime, show it, and drop it and the nickel into your pocket.

11. Do the same with the second dime. "How many coins in my left hand?" you ask.

12. Wait for the answers, then say, "One coin, twenty-five cents," and slap the quarter on the table.

IMPORTANT POINTS: The most important part of the entire routine is when you drop a visible and a secret coin together into your left hand. As your right hand approaches the left, start slowly closing your left fingers. For a split second, as the secret coin drops, the tips of the fingers of both hands slightly overlap so the coins can't be seen. Then, by the time your right hand has withdrawn, the left fingers are closed and your audience doesn't know you've sneaked a second coin into your hand.

RIGHT THROUGH

EFFECT: You show a half-dollar and put it into the center of a handkerchief. After showing that the coin really is underneath the cloth, you then proceed to bring the coin right through the center.

PROPS NEEDED: A half-dollar, a handkerchief

SECRET: It's all in the way you manipulate the handkerchief and the coin.

ROUTINE: 1. Hold a half-dollar at the tips of your left fingers and drape the handkerchief over it, making sure that one corner of the handkerchief is on your left arm and pointing toward your elbow.

MONEY MAGIC

2. As you adjust the cloth over the coin, your right thumb holds the cloth against the back of the coin while your left thumb leaves the coin and comes back to pinch a bit of the cloth against the back of the coin.

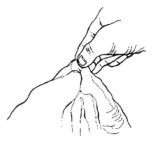

3. "Look," you say, "I want you to be sure that the coin is really under the cloth." Your right hand picks up the corner that's hanging in front of your left hand and lifts it up to show your left hand holding the coin. Actually, your right hand brings its corner of the cloth back so it's directly over the corner on your left arm and your right thumb secretly picks up that corner.

4. Now sweep the cloth forward and down to cover the coin again, but this time bringing both corners to the front so, as you straighten the folds of the cloth, the coin is actually outside the handkerchief and hidden in a pocket behind the center of the hank.

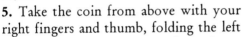

5. Take the coin from above with your right fingers and thumb, folding the left and right sides of the cloth to the back to completely enfold the coin. This will make the shape of the coin very obvious and you can rap it against the table.

6. "Watch!" you say.
Your right fingers again take the coin from above, your right thumb goes down into the folds of cloth, and you pull the coin right up and away from the handkerchief.

7. Drop the coin on the table and spread the handkerchief out to show that there aren't any holes in it.

COPPER/SILVER THROUGH

EFFECT: You put a half-dollar and a large copper coin inside a handkerchief and wrap them securely. Someone names one of the coins and you magically pull it right through the cloth.

PROPS NEEDED: Two half-dollars, an old British penny, a handkerchief

SECRET: You use a second half-dollar as a stand-in for the one that's visible. The copper coin is an old English penny, one that was current before 1971 when they changed their monetary system from pounds/shillings/pence to a decimal system, and that penny is the same size as a half-dollar. You can find them at almost any coin store, they're not expensive and they come in very handy for any number of coin tricks.

ROUTINE: 1. With one of the half-dollars concealed in your left hand, your right hand puts the other half and the English penny on the table, along with a handkerchief.

2. Drape the handkerchief over your left hand. Put the half-dollar in the center of it, but so it overlaps the lower edge of the penny under the cloth.

3. Pick up the visible penny and put it on top of the visible half, so it overlaps the upper edge of that coin.

4. Now pick up the corner of the handkerchief at the back and bring it over the coins and down in front. "Remember, two coins-one copper and one silver."

5. As you say that, pick up the front corner of the cloth and bring it back over the two coins to show them. As you take that corner back down in front, your left thumb and first finger grip the upper edges of the hidden half-dollar and penny so the half-dollar inside the handkerchief can drop into your right fingers.

6. Hold that coin by slightly curling your middle two fingers then reach up and fold the left side of the handkerchief around and behind the hidden half-dollar, so the shape of the two coins shows through the cloth.

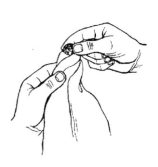

7. "I want you to name either of the two coins, either the silver or the copper."

As you say that, you have plenty of opportunity to get rid of the coin in your right hand by dropping it into your right jacket pocket, into the hip pocket of your pants, or into your shirt collar at the back of your neck.

8. When they answer with the name of a coin, you then use magician's choice to pro-

duce the half-dollar. That is, if they name silver, then you tell them that you'll magically penetrate the silver coin right through the cloth, leaving the copper penny inside the handkerchief. If, on the other hand, they name the copper coin, you say that's the coin they'll get.
9. In any case, you reach over to the two coins with your right hand and while grasping the cloth below the coins with your left hand, you work the half-dollar out of its pocket behind the screen of your right fingers and drop it on the table. Now hand the handkerchief to someone so they can find the penny still inside.

TEN PENNY VANISH
(Thomas A. Silliman)

EFFECT: You have ten pennies in your open left hand and you have someone hold out their open hand. One at a time you count the pennies into their hand, dropping the last one in from your left hand, and they close their fingers. When they squeeze the coins back into your hands, however, there are only nine pennies. You repeat the trick, dropping each coin separately into their hand, but when they count them back again, there are only eight.
PROPS NEEDED: Ten pennies
SECRET: It's all in the way you handle the pennies and it isn't difficult.
ROUTINE: 1. Have the ten pennies scattered out on the palm of your open left hand and have someone hold their hand out, palm-up and open.
2. You say to them, "I'm going to count these pennies into your hand one at a time, except for the last one. I'm just going to drop the last one into your hand and I want you to close your fingers around it as soon as it hits your hand."
3. Hold your left hand just to the left of their hand and slightly above it. With your right thumb and first finger, pick up a penny and place it in their palm.
4. You keep doing the same move with each penny, counting out loud for each one and making sure that each penny clinks down on the growing pile, EXCEPT for the ninth one.
5. The ninth penny you pick up, count out loud as you carry it to their hand, and you just push it against the other pennies, but you don't let go of it.

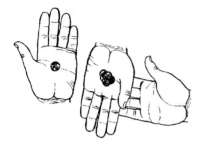

6. You now raise your left hand up so it's about six inches above their hand and at the same time, you move your right hand under their hand, straightening out your fingers as you do so. With the ninth penny hidden on the tips of your right fingers, no one can see it. You can even touch the coin against the back of their hand and they can't tell the difference between the coin and the tips of your fingers. Put your fingertips under their hand just far enough to conceal the coin and to let everyone see that your empty right palm is showing.

7. Drop the last penny into their hand and have them close their fingers immediately. Drop your right hand to your side with the penny resting on your open and curled fingers.

8. "Now, how many do you have? Ten, that's right. I want you to squeeze those coins out of your fingers, one at a time, counting them as you do so, and let them drop into my hand."

9. As they're dropping the pennies into your left hand, your right hand gets rid of its penny. How you do this depends completely on your circumstances. You can drop it into a pants pocket, your side jacket pocket, down the back of your neck, or into your lap if you're seated at a table. The main thing is to get rid of it before your helper counts out the ninth and last penny so that both of your hands are empty and back in sight.

10. "Only nine? What did you do with the other one? Well, let's do it again and this time keep track of each one."

11. Repeat the trick, move for move, making your stealing move on the eighth penny, and they'll be more mystified than the first time.

12. Repeat the trick one more time then put the pennies back in your pocket with the remark, "I'd better stop before I lose all of them."

IMPORTANT POINTS: Both of your hands move at the same time when you steal the next-to-last penny and raise your left hand to drop the last one in their hand. They'll be watching your left hand to make sure that they'll be able to catch the last penny, but everyone can see that your right hand is apparently empty. This is an excellent trick to do for children that are between the ages of five and ten, as they like to count and it's a simple routine to understand.

DIGITAL DOLLARS
(Karl Fulves)

EFFECT: This is a trick that can also be done over a telephone, as well as just having your back turned while you're in the same room with your audience.

Have someone take a one-dollar bill, a five-dollar bill, and a ten-dollar bill from their wallet and put them in a row on the table in any order. Ask him if he's willing to bet five dollars on the outcome of the experiment. You're going to have him move the bills around without him saying a word and at the end, you have to pick out the ten-dollar bill without asking him any questions in order to win your bet.

PROPS NEEDED: You don't need anything, but the person helping you will need a one-dollar bill, a five-dollar bill, and a ten-dollar bill.

SECRET: It's all in the way you have him move the bills and in the end, you can always pick out the bill of the highest denomination.

ROUTINE: 1. The bills have been laid out in any order and you want him to move the bills, one at a time, just as you direct. At no time is he to tell you anything.
2. Have him exchange the one-dollar bill with the bill to the right of it. If there isn't any bill to the right, then he leaves all the bills as they are.
3. Now he's to exchange the ten-dollar bill with the bill to the left of it and he doesn't do anything if there isn't a bill there.
4. Finally, he's to exchange the five-dollar bill with the bill to the right of it. If there's no bill, he does nothing.
5. You remind him that you have to pick the five-dollar bill to at least break even and so you have to find the ten-dollar bill to make any money. When he agrees, you ask for the bill at the left end of the row and you win.

IMPORTANT POINTS: The moves you make are with the one, the ten, and the five, in that order, and those bills are to be exchanged with the bills at their right, their left, and their right, in that order. At the end, the highest denomination bill will always be at the left end. Name that bill as being on the left and collect your winnings later.

TWO FOR TWO

EFFECT: You show your audience a two-dollar bill, making sure that they realize that you have just the one bill. A few quick folds and

you suddenly have two one-dollar bills. You unfold them and you now have just one one-dollar bill.

PROPS NEEDED: A one-dollar bill and a two-dollar bill

SECRET: You actually have one gimmicked bill that becomes disguised as all the other combinations.

PREPARATION: Go to the bank and get a new two-dollar bill and a new one-dollar bill. When you get home glue the two bills together back-to-back so the portrait sides are to the outside and with both bills right side up.

Now hold the bill(s) so you're looking at the one-dollar side and fold the bill along its length and with the top of the bill folding away from you. Crease the fold to make sure it has a good memory. Open it up and fold the bill across its center, from top to bottom, with the right end going away from you. Crease it and open it out.

Now fold the right end toward you and up so the fold goes right through the center, but not at a right angle; the lower edge of the bill should slant to the right when the fold is flattened. Crease the fold and open the bill.

Now, hold the bill with George Washington looking at you and start to fold the bill lengthwise at the same time that you bend both ends down and toward each other. When the folds go flat, you will have what looks like two one-dollar bills folded in half and being held in a V-shape.

Open the bill out and put it in your wallet flat and with the two-dollar side facing up.

ROUTINE: 1. Hold the bill with the two-dollar side toward your audience and snap it a couple of times to show that it's only one bill.

2. Hold it horizontally between your two hands and bend the top and bottom toward your audience so that they only see the two-dollar side becoming the two edges of the bill. Just before the two edges meet, push the ends towards each other to form the V and switch your right thumb and first finger to the top of the V. Swivel the bill between those fingertips at the same time that you tip the bill forward and it now looks as though you have two bills folded in half.

3. Turn your hand to show the other sides of the "bills" and bring it back again.

4. Bring your left hand over, slip the tip of your first finger into the top fold of the bills, and open up the fold between your two hands to show only one one-dollar bill.

5. Snap it a couple of times and put it back in your wallet.

IMPORTANT POINTS: Practice the folding move in front of a mirror until you're sure that your audience won't see a two-dollar face and a one-dollar face at the same time.

At the end, the opening of the folds so the two bills become a single one-dollar bill has to be immediate and without hesitation to look its best.

DOLLAR CHANGE
(Lou Tannen)

EFFECT: A dollar bill is placed in an envelope, the envelope sealed to keep the bill inside, and the envelope is cut in half. When the two halves of the envelope are opened, however, the bill is gone and two half-dollars fall out.

PROPS NEEDED: Two half-dollars, ten to twelve #7 coin envelopes, some soft wax, a pair of scissors

SECRET: The first envelope is switched for a second one with the half-dollars inside.

PREPARATION: From a stationery store buy some #7 coin envelopes that are 3 1/2" by 6 1/2" in size. Take one envelope and put a small dab of soft wax or Tac'N Stik on the center of each of the two half-dollars. Slide one half inside the envelope so the wax is against the inside of the face of the envelope and when it gets all the way to the bottom, press the face of the envelope against the coin to make it stick. The second waxed half goes inside the envelope so it's just inside the flap before it's stuck against the inside of the face.

Put this envelope on a stack of about eight others, all of which have their flaps sticking out. Another envelope has its flap cut off and is put on top of the coin envelope so their ends are absolutely even. A rubber

HOUDINI'S SCHOOL OF MAGIC

band is put around the whole stack. Have a pair of scissors handy.

ROUTINE: 1. Borrow a one-dollar bill as you tell your audience that you've discovered a way to make money indestructible.

2. Slide the bill into the top envelope (the flapless one), take the flap of the next envelope, and pull that one out and away from the stack. Drop the envelopes face down on the table as you reach for the scissors.

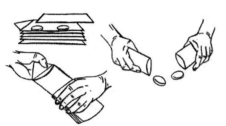

3. Seal the flap of the envelope and hold it in a flat, horizontal position in front of you.

4. Cut through the center of the envelope, and then take one half in each hand.

5. Squeeze on the top and bottom folds of the halves to open them up. The coins will separate from the inside of the paper and fall out onto the table.

6. "I've just made two halves out of a whole one," you tell your audience as you give them to the person who loaned you the bill.

ONE, TWO, THREE, MAGIC!

Working with puzzles does more for you than just killing time or having fun. Puzzles can show you new ways to look at the world around you, demonstrate some of the peculiar ways that numbers work, help you learn how to think logically, and teach you how to solve hard problems with easy methods. So, when someone gives you a puzzle to solve, don't just give up on it; see if you can solve the mystery by looking at in a different way.

PUZZLE: Can you draw the next shape in this series?
Before we give you the correct answer (and there's only one correct

answer), let's explore the world of puzzles.

What is a puzzle?

Most people think that it's only a game or toy to test your ingenuity like a trick question. But many problems can be called puzzles. For centuries people watched birds fly and wondered how it was done. That was a puzzle. Slowly, different methods and theories were tried until one day we could fly. We not only can fly, but we can do it faster and farther than the birds that started us thinking.

Thinking.

That's what solves puzzling problems and sometimes it takes a little longer than we expect. Like the puzzle we just gave you. Do the symbols look familiar at all? Maybe they're disguised. Try covering the left half of each one and see what you find.

Did you see the digits from 1 to 7? Well, that's what they are. Each one has a mirror image attached to its left side. That means the

HOUDINI'S SCHOOL OF MAGIC

next symbol should be an 8, doubled. What does that look like?

After solving that, maybe you'll start seeing the world a little differently. Artists do-they see everything around them as shapes and combinations of colors. Fashion designers see people's shapes and sizes and figure out how to make them look better or different. Each of them can look at the same scene, but will be thinking of different ways to rearrange it. Here's a puzzle for you to arrange:

PUZZLE: Place the digits from 1 to 9 in the nine blank spaces of this problem so it adds up correctly:

If that problem takes you a little time to solve, here's another one to do while you're thinking.

PUZZLE: What is the meaning of this number?

8 5 4 9 1 7 6 3 2 0

Does the fact that it doesn't have any commas mean anything? Notice that no digits are duplicated. Maybe it looks strange because they're in a particular order. Try looking at the puzzle like this:

Eight, Five, Four, Nine, One. . .

Do you see it yet?

SECRET: The digits are in alphabetical order.

We get so used to looking at digits as parts of numbers, that we tend to forget that they're also words. Incidentally, the answer to that problem in addition up above is to add four hundred and twenty-nine to one hundred and thirty-eight in order to get a total of five hundred and sixty-seven. Aren't numbers amazing?

Money is made of numbers and we usually think of it as being certain values. That is, we think of pennies, dimes, dollar bills, and ten-dollar bills. Thinking of money that way, can you solve the next mystery?

PUZZLE: If a man has six coins that total $1.15, and he can't change a dollar bill or any other coin, what six coins does he have?

Now the hardest part of the question is where it says that he can't give change for another coin. That means he can't have two dimes and a nickel, because then he could change a quarter; and he can't have five pennies or he could change a nickel. Can you figure it out?

While you're working on that, try this easy one:

PUZZLE: Arrange three 8s so they equal 9.

Think about it real hard, because it must be done in a way that you're not used to doing. Like when you work with fractions, you always change improper fractions to whole numbers. Does that give you a hint?

ONE, TWO, THREE, MAGIC!

The man with the money also had a problem of whole coins making up fractions of a dollar. If you figured out the answer, you'd know that he had one half-dollar, one quarter, and four dimes. That totals one dollar and fifteen cents, but he can't give change for any coins. The answer to the problem of three 8s is much simpler. Just think of nine as being eight and eight-eighths! Now that you know that, answer this:

PUZZLE: Arrange eight 8s to equal 1,000.

Learning about the strange ways that numbers work with each other can be a big help in everyday life. Did you ever hear about the boy taking an arithmetic test and he had the following problems?

1 x 9 =
2 x 9 =
3 x 9 =
4 x 9 =
5 x 9 =
6 x 9 =
7 x 9 =
8 x 9 =
9 x 9 =

He said to himself, "Now I know that the answer to the first problem is 9," so he wrote it down. The other eight problems stumped him, however, and he decided to find out just how many of them he would miss. So, he counted them, numbering them as he went -

1 x 9 = 9
2 x 9 = 1
3 x 9 = 2
4 x 9 = 3
5 x 9 = 4
6 x 9 = 5
7 x 9 = 6
8 x 9 = 7
9 x 9 = 8

"Will I really miss eight of them?" he asked himself. "Maybe I'd better count them again." So he did, this time from the bottom up.

1 x 9 = 9
2 x 9 = 18
3 x 9 = 27
4 x 9 = 36

HOUDINI'S SCHOOL OF MAGIC

$$5 \times 9 = 45$$
$$6 \times 9 = 54$$
$$7 \times 9 = 63$$
$$8 \times 9 = 72$$
$$9 \times 9 = 81$$

He decided it was all too much for him, turned in his test paper, and was very surprised when it was returned to him marked "100%"!

He also didn't know that you can arrange eight 8s to make a thousand by doing this -

```
    888
     88
      8
      8
 +    8
  1,000
```

There's an old saying, "Figures don't lie." But there's another one saying, "You can make numbers prove anything," and it's probably been around as long as the first one. The following is a good demonstration for that last proverb. Learn to do this quickly and you can really confuse people.

"If seven vacuum cleaner salesmen have a total of 28 vacuums to sell, then each salesman has to sell 13 vacuum cleaners, right? Look, I'll prove it:

"We'll multiply 13 by 7"
7 times 3 equals 21 right?
7 times 1 equals 7 right?
And 21 plus 7 equals 28 right?

"All right, then suppose we divide."

7 can't go into 2
But 7 does go into 8 once
Subtract the 7
And 7 goes into 21 three times
So, 7 goes into 28 thirteen times!

"You still don't believe me? Okay, now to prove it.

Add 13 seven times.
"Seven 3s are 21, right?
And seven 1s equal 7, right?
That means that seven 13s equal 28!"

So you see, you really can make numbers prove almost anything! But, first of all, you have to understand how numbers work. Since each number can represent only one value, and when we count we keep repeating the same numbers the same number of times, we then create cycles. This means that certain digits will keep reappearing at certain times. Both bookkeepers and mathematicians use these principles all the time. The number 9 is very impressive in the many ways that it keeps popping up. For example-

PUZZLE: Take any two-digit number from 10 to 99, add those two digits together then subtract that answer from your original two-digit number. Add together the two digits of the answer, and I can tell you your final answer.

SECRET: The answer is 9 and will always be (unless your helper makes a mistake in the arithmetic).

Here are two more impressive ways that the number 9 is remarkable.

$$0 \times 9 + 1 = 1$$
$$1 \times 9 + 2 = 11$$
$$12 \times 9 + 3 = 111$$
$$123 \times 9 + 4 = 1,111$$
$$1,234 \times 9 + 5 = 11,111$$
$$12,345 \times 9 + 6 = 111,111$$
$$123,456 \times 9 + 7 = 1,111,111$$
$$1,234,567 \times 9 + 8 = 11,111,111$$
$$12,345,678 \times 9 + 9 = 111,111,111$$

- Or -

$$0 \times 9 + 8 = 8$$
$$9 \times 9 + 7 = 88$$
$$98 \times 9 + 6 = 888$$
$$987 \times 9 + 5 = 8,888$$
$$9,876 \times 9 + 4 = 88,888$$
$$98,765 \times 9 + 3 = 888,888$$

HOUDINI'S SCHOOL OF MAGIC

$$987{,}654 \times 9 + 2 = 8{,}888{,}888$$
$$9{,}876{,}543 \times 9 + 1 = 88{,}888{,}888$$
$$98{,}765{,}432 \times 9 + 0 = 888{,}888{,}888$$

Plus, after all that work, if you add the answers of the first problem to the answers of the second problem, you again get a lot of 9s!

If you're tired of numbers by now, then try this:

PUZZLE: What does this group of letters mean?
O T T F F S S E N

Look at all the things you've learned just by trying to solve puzzles. Puzzles of different kinds are around us every day and everywhere. We can trade puzzles with our friends and find them in books and magazines, as well as in the work and play that we do. And if you've given up on that last puzzle, just look at them again and count, "One, Two, Three."

The following three puzzles should be in every magician's file as they can be used as a braintwister when someone asks you to do a trick and you don't have a deck of cards with you. You can also have them printed on the back of your business cards so people will be more apt to remember you.

In each one, you substitute one of the digits from 0 to 9 for each letter and follow the multiplication or addition to arrive at the correct answer. The first one adds HOCUS to POCUS to arrive at PRESTO and the second one is CIGAM multiplied by 4 to get MAGIC. The third one might be a telegram from a magician to his agent, and by adding SEND to MORE you find out just how much MONEY he needs.

```
   HOCUS           CIGAM           SEND
  +POCUS            x 4           + MORE
  ─────            ─────          ──────
  PRESTO           MAGIC          MONEY
```

(The answers will be found at the end of the chapter)

A good magician is able to perform tricks with anything that is around; it's not necessary to have boxes or tubes or special pieces of equipment. The real test of a magician's skills is when ordinary objects surround you. Take a calendar, for instance. There are some very intriguing tricks you can do with a page from a calendar.

ONE, TWO, THREE, MAGIC!

THREE IN A ROW

EFFECT: While your back is turned, someone circles three dates in a row anywhere on the calendar. They add the three dates together and give you the total. Immediately, you name the three dates they circled.

PROPS NEEDED: A calendar page A pen or pencil

SECRET: When they give you the total, all you do is mentally divide that number by 3. This will give you the center number of the three dates; subtracting 1 from that number then gives you the first of the three dates and you count forward from there.

For example, let's say that someone gives you 45 as their total. When you divide that 45 by 3, you get 15 as the middle number. Subtract 1 from 15 and you get 14. So 14, 15, and 16 are the three dates that your friend circled on the calendar.

IMPORTANT POINTS: By looking at those three dates on any calendar page you can reason out why the trick works. If you subtract 1 from the third date and add it to the first date you'll get the same three numbers in a row. Therefore, the center date will always be one-third of the total of the three dates.

One of the rules of magic, though, is not to let your audience get a chance to think about what you did or they may find the simple answer. So quickly follow your first mystery with a second one.

SQUARE OF FOUR

EFFECT: Someone draws a square around a block of four dates on any page of a calendar, like the 10, 11, 17, and 18. They quietly add the four dates together and give you the total. You then tell them the four dates they used.

PROPS NEEDED: A calendar page A pen or pencil

SECRET: The easy way to remember how to do this trick is that it involves three 4s. They draw a square around four dates, then you divide their total by 4, and you subtract 4 from that answer.

159

When you do that, you have the first number of the four dates. Add 1 to that date to get the second date. For the other two dates, you add 6 to the second date and name the following number after that for the last date circled.

Let's say that the total given to you is 96. When you secretly divide that total by 4, you get 24. When you subtract 4 from 24, you get 20, the first of the four dates. The following number is the second date and when you add 6 to that number you get 27 as the third number. The following number is the last of the four. So your answer is 20, 21, 27, and 28.

SQUARE OF NINE

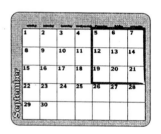

EFFECT: This time someone draws a square around nine dates, with three dates on each side of the square. When they give you the smallest date (for example, 5) you give them the total of all nine dates (in this case, 117).

PROPS NEEDED: A calendar page. A pen or pencil

SECRET: Take the number they give you, add 8, and multiply the answer by 9 to get the sum of all nine dates.

In our example, you were given 5, so 5 plus 8 equal 13, and when you multiply 13 by 9 you get 117. Aren't you glad you know your multiplication tables?

A DIFFERENT VERSION

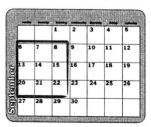

EFFECT: Again have nine dates marked off in a square, three dates on a side. This time, however, all the person has to do is give you the total of the smallest and largest dates. Let's say they tell you 28. You then tell them that the nine squares that are inside the square are the 6, 7, 8, 13, 14, 15, 20, 21, and 22.

PROPS NEEDED: A calendar page. A pen or pencil

ONE, TWO, THREE, MAGIC!

SECRET: This mystery looks difficult, but it's as easy as the first one you learned. Take their total, 28, and divide it by 2. You get 14, the date in the center of the nine numbers. By subtracting 8 from this date, you get the first date of the first row, in this case 6. You now know that the first row is made up of 6, 7, and 8. By adding 5 to the last number of that group, the 8, you get 13, the first number of the second row: 13, 14, and 15. Now by adding 5 to the 15 you get 20 for the first number of the last row of three dates.

IMPORTANT POINTS: Here's the formula: Divide their total by 2. Subtract 8 from your answer to get the first number of the first row. Add 5 to the last number to get the first number of the second row. Add 5 to the last number to get the first number of the third row.

ELIMINATION

EFFECT: This time you apparently demonstrate that you not only can juggle numbers in your head, but that you can also predict what someone else will do. Give someone a page from a calendar and have them draw a square 3 by 3 or 4 by 4. As soon as they do so, you immediately write a number in one corner of the page. Give them back the pencil, tell them to circle any date inside their square, and cross out all the other dates in the row and the column in which that date appears. For example, if they circled the 17, they would cross out all the following dates: 14, 15, 16, 10, 24, and 31.

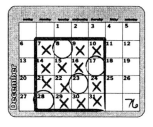

They then circle any of the dates left and again cross out the other dates in that row and column. This continues until only one date remains and it's circled. All the circled dates are added together and the total matches the prediction you wrote in the corner of the page.

PROPS NEEDED: A calendar page. A pen or pencil

SECRET: The secrets for working with squares using three and four dates on a side are very simple. For a three-date square, multiply the center date by 3. For a square with four dates on each side, add together either pair of dates that are

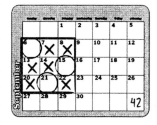

diagonally opposite. For example, in the following square, you can add together either the 7 and the 31, or the 10 and 28. In either case, you then double your answer to get your prediction.

ROUTINE: Hand the page and pencil to someone and ask them to draw a square around a group of dates so they have three or four dates on each side. As soon as they've done that, do your quick calculation as you ask for the pencil. Write your total in one corner of the page, and then give back the pencil. They now circle any date inside their square and cross out all the other numbers in that column and row. They continue to do this until all they have is four circled numbers. When they add those four numbers their total will match your prediction.

MAGIC MNEMONICS

Your first question is "What are mnemonics?" It's actually a Greek word, pronounced like "ne-moniks", and we use it to describe the various systems that help us remember things. Sometimes we use a single word to help us remember a number of objects like using the acronym ROY G BIV to remember the colors of a rainbow in proper order: red, orange, yellow, green, blue, indigo, and violet.

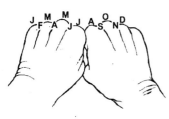

Other times we use something entirely different to help us remember certain information. For instance, if you can't remember if there are 30 or 31 days in a month there is a simpler method than looking at a calendar. Make two fists, hold them out in front of you with your thumbs together, and look at your knuckles. Start with your left little finger knuckle, and think of it as January. Now move down into the dip between the two knuckles and call that February. The knuckle for your left ring finger is March, the next dip is April, and so on. All of your knuckle-months have 31 days, and the others 30, except for February, of course.

Why are we talking about mnemonics in a magic book? Because most highly skilled magicians use some sort of mnemonic system to remember a great variety of lists, and the earlier you learn a system the easier it gets as you learn more magic. Most of the mnemonic systems use a number base that is turned into words because you can remember words more easily than numbers. Since we want you to start learn-

ONE, TWO, THREE, MAGIC!

ing with an easy system, we'll skip the number system and just use a list of objects as our basic mnemonic system. First of all, look at the following list of ten simple keywords that rhyme with the numbers they represent:

One	Gun
Two	Shoe
Three	Flea
Four	Door
Five	Hive
Six	Tricks
Seven	Raven
Eight	Gate
Nine	Sign
Ten	Pen

Now we're going to give you a more complex list of ten random objects and show you how easy it is to memorize it. First of all, here is the list:

1 - Book
2 - Pencil
3 - Car
4 - Duck
5 - Ball
6 - Bicycle
7 - Computer
8 - Desk
9 - Feather
10 - Penny

The object is to make a picture in your mind that connects the object at each number with your memorized keyword for that number. Use your imagination and make the following pictures in your mind as we describe them:

A gun shooting through a book.
You're writing on the floor with a pencil that's tied to your shoe.
A little flea pulling a big car.
A door has just slammed on Donald Duck and he's flat.
Bees trying to stuff a beach ball into a hive. A magician doing tricks while standing on a bicycle.

A raven picking at the keys of a computer.
A desk swinging on a fence like a gate.
Someone painting a big sign using a little feather.
You're writing your name on the edge of a penny with a pen.

Have you done that? Now cover up the list of objects and the list of pictures and just look at the first list, the list of keywords. When you look at any one of those objects you will recall the picture in your mind and can name the object you've associated with the basic key. For example, look at "Raven" and you should see one of those birds pecking away in front of a computer.

Now look just at the numbers from one to ten and see if you can recall both the keyword and the memorized object.

After memorizing your basic list of ten keywords, have someone give you a list of any ten objects they can see in the room. Again, make a vivid picture of each keyword reacting with the object at that number on their list and you'll find you can memorize the list in a very short time.

Using this list of keywords you can now memorize grocery lists, things you have to do during the day, or even objects you have to take with you on a trip. And, now that you understand how real mnemonic systems work, let's show you some tricky memory feats.

PLAYING CARD MEMORY

EFFECT: Showing a mixed-up deck of cards, you tell a friend that you've memorized all fifty-two cards from top to bottom. To prove it, you're going to have one card removed, and you'll name it. After a card is removed, you look through the rest of the deck and correctly name the card.
PROPS NEEDED: A deck of cards
SECRET: The deck is actually arranged, or stacked, in a special order, and that order will tell you which card is missing.
PREPARATION: Put any card face up on the table and subtract the value of that card from 13. Let's say you have the Nine of Hearts face up. When you subtract 9 from 13 you get 4, so you now look for the Four that is the same color but the other suit; that is, the Four of Diamonds. When you find it you put it face up on top of the Nine. Put any other card face-up on the Four, and follow the same formula: subtract its value from 13 and find the card of that value and of the

other suit of that same color. Remember to count Jacks as 11, Queens as 12, and the Kings as 13. The Kings, of course, are placed by themselves between any of the pairs.

Since you're dealing the first card of each pair randomly from the remainder of the deck, you'll have both large and small groups of cards of the same color, and the values will be mixed. Put the deck in its box and you're ready to work.

ROUTINE: 1. Remove the deck from the case as you explain that you've memorized the order of the deck and spread it face up on the table so everyone can see that it's apparently well-mixed.
2. Pick it up, turn it face down, cut it a few times to apparently make it more difficult, and hand it to someone.
3. They remove any card and put it to one side facedown. Cut the deck once or twice and give it back to you.
4. Taking the deck, you look at the top and bottom cards to see if they belong together as a pair and then go on through the deck to check each pair of cards. You will find one of two possible results.
5. One, if all the pairs are still together, then the selected card is one of the Kings, and you quickly run through the cards to see which one is missing.
6. Two, there will be one card that doesn't have a partner. In that case, subtract its value from 13, and name that value with the other suit of that color. For example, if you find the Jack of Diamonds all by itself, then you know that the missing card is the Two of Hearts.

MEMORIZING A DECK
(Martin Sunshine)

EFFECT: A deck is shuffled by someone, and then they deal cards off the top of the pack, one at a time, naming them while you stand with your back turned so you can't see the cards. After eighteen or twenty cards have been named, the pile of face-up cards is replaced on top of the deck and it's given to you.

You hold the deck behind your back so no one can accuse you of peeking at the cards, and ask for a number between one and eight. When the number is given, you name a card and bring the deck forward. You count down to that number, turn over the card, and it's the one you named. The cards are replaced, the deck again goes behind your back, and a number between seven and fifteen is named. Again, you name a card and it is shown to be correct. You also name a card for any number between twelve and wherever you stopped memorizing the cards.

PROPS NEEDED: A deck of cards

SECRET: You actually memorize the cards! You don't, however, memorize all twenty cards that are named only three of them. Count the cards as they're named and memorize the fifth, tenth, and fifteenth cards. It's easy as all you do is mentally repeat the names of the three cards over and over as you do the rest of the trick. You always memorize the fifth, tenth, and fifteenth cards when you do the trick so you don't have to remember the positions, you already know them.

ROUTINE: 1. Give the deck to someone and ask him or her to shuffle it. When that's done, explain that you're going to memorize the top twenty cards of the deck, so you want the person to turn the cards over, one at a time, naming them as they do so. You're going to turn your back to the cards so you only get one chance to remember each card.

2. As the cards are named, memorize the fifth, tenth, and fifteenth cards, and then stop the dealing after the person passes the twentieth card.

3. Have the face-up cards dropped back onto the deck and the deck given to you. Put it behind your back, or under the table, and hold it between your two hands.

4. Ask for a number from one to eight. When one is named, name the card that is fifth from the top, and then add or subtract cards from the top to make the number come out. For example, let's say they name four as the number. You would immediately take the top card off the deck and put it on the bottom. Your memorized card is now fourth from the top. Bring the deck forward, count off four cards, turn over the last card dealt, and it's your memorized card. Put the cards back onto the deck, put the deck behind your back, and take the card from the bottom and put it back on top. Your setup is back in order.

5. Let's say that for the next number, from seven to fifteen, that someone says twelve. Your next card is the tenth one from the top, so as you name it you add two cards from the bottom of the pack to the top. Bring out the deck, deal off the number, and show the correct card. Reassemble the deck, put it behind your back, and take two cards off the top and put them back on the bottom.

6. You do the same for the third card for any number between twelve and twenty.

IMPORTANT POINT: Don't forget to readjust the deck every time

ONE, TWO, THREE, MAGIC!

you put it back behind you. You have to put your arrangement back in the order that you remember it.

This is a perfect trick to follow "Playing Card Memory" as all you have to do at the end of that trick is hand the deck out for shuffling, and then go through this routine to show how fast you can memorize cards.

MAGIC SQUARES

A Magic Square is a series of numbers arranged so they always add up to a certain total for each column, each row, and each of the two diagonals. No one knows how long people have been making magic squares as they've been found in ancient Chinese graves, drawn on the walls of extinct cities, and written about in antique manuscripts. For centuries artists, scientists, mathematicians, and the average man have studied them.

Before we start learning a couple of squares, let's talk about their parts:

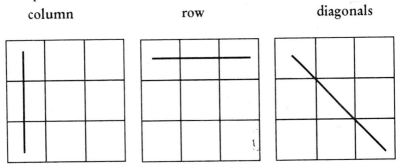

column   **row**   **diagonals**

The entire figure is known as the **SQUARE**

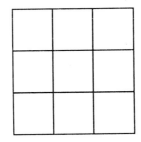

HOUDINI'S SCHOOL OF MAGIC

Each smaller square is known as a **CELL**

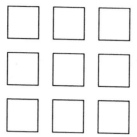

You can make magic squares that are very simple, or very complicated. Benjamin Franklin made one that was made up of 256 cells, sixteen cells on each side, and each of the rows, columns, and any square of 16 cells added up to a grand total of 2,056. Unfortunately, it hasn't survived and we don't know how long it took him to put it together.

The simplest magic square is made up of nine cells, three columns of three rows each. Can you arrange the digits from 1 to 9 in the following square so that each row, each column, and each diagonal adds up to 15?

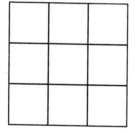

If not, here is how you figure out the answer: When you write the digits of 1 to 9 in a row, the 5 is the middle digit, that is, there are four digits on each side of it. Now, when you put the 5 in the center cell of the square, the other digits can be put around it so that each of the larger numbers will balance two of the ones that are less in value. There are eight ways to arrange the digits from 1 to 9 in that square, and here's just one of the ways to do it -

8	1	6
3	5	7
4	9	2

Can you make another square by putting them in a slightly different order?

SIXTEEN-CELL SQUARE

The nine-cell square is called an odd-order square because its sides are made up of three cells each and three is an odd number. We'll now work with an even-order square, a sixteen-cell square with four cells on each side.

Here is the basic sixteen-cell square using the numbers from 1 to 16:

14	1	12	7
11	8	13	2
5	10	3	16
4	15	6	9

Notice that this square adds up to 34 in twenty-four different ways:

The rows	4 ways
The columns	4 ways
The diagonals	2 ways
The four corners	1 way
Squares of four cells	9 ways
The center two cells of each side plus the two on the opposite side	2 ways
Diagonal squares in each corner	2 ways
	24 ways

Notice, also, that in each group of four consecutive digits (1,2,3,4 - 5,6,7,8 - 9,10,11,12 - 13,14,15,16) that no two of the same group are in the same row or column. This is how this magic square is kept in balance.

But how do we make a mystery out of this interesting bit of mathematical manipulation?

EFFECT: Someone names a number, or their age, as you draw the

HOUDINI'S SCHOOL OF MAGIC

sixteen-cell square. You write their number outside the square then fill in the squares as fast as you can write. When finished each column, diagonal, row, and the four corners add up to the named number.

SECRET: All you have to do is figure out numbers for four of the cells, all the others you have memorized. First of all, memorize the position of which cells use the numbers of 1 to 12. The formula for working out the remaining four cells is as follows:

Their selected number minus 20 goes into the x cell

x	1	12	7
11	8	$x-1$	2
5	10	3	$x+2$
4	$x+1$	6	9

which is the first cell you fill in with your pencil. Then you put the correct numbers in the next five cells which brings you to the $x-1$ cell, so you subtract 1 from the number in the first cell and write it in here. Continue on, adding the proper amounts for the other two x cells, and when you finish you can add up the eleven different ways that the square adds up to the selected number. Here's what it will look like if the number is **43**

23	1	12	7
11	8	22	2
5	10	3	25
4	24	6	9

IMPORTANT POINTS: There are two points to remember. One, the number selected by the spectator should be over 21, otherwise you'll be working with negative numbers and that gets complicated. That's why someone's age is a good selection.

Two, when the number they choose is a multiple of 4 (24, 28, 32, etc.), you can now make the square add up in the basic 24 different ways rather than just 11.

ONE, TWO, THREE, MAGIC!

ANSWERS TO THE THREE MAGIC PUZZLES:

92836	21978	9567
12836	x4	1085
105672	87912	10652

BALANCING WATER

EFFECT: While seated at a dining table, you pick up your water tumbler and very carefully balance it on its bottom edge so it's at a dangerous angle.
PROPS NEEDED: A large round toothpick or wooden match
PREPARATION: Sometime, before dinner starts, you have to smuggle the match or toothpick under the tablecloth to where you're going to balance the glass later.
ROUTINE: 1. Smooth out the tablecloth so you know exactly where the hidden match is located.
2. Hold your glass, which should be half full of water, at an angle and place it on the tablecloth next to the match. Push the bottom of the glass against the match and adjust the balance of the glass until it can stand by itself.

HOUDINI CARD

EFFECT: After showing a playing card with a hole in the center, you put the card into a coin envelope and then seal it shut. You then push a needle that is threaded with yarn through the center of the envelope and have someone hold both ends of the yarn. Cutting off the bottom of the envelope, you reach in and remove the card, leaving the envelope still threaded on the yarn.
PROPS NEEDED: A #7 coin envelope, an old playing card, a darning needle, yarn that fits the eye of the needle
SECRET: Cut a slit in the bottom of the envelope so the card can be secretly slid part-

way out of the envelope.

PREPARATION: Cut a half-inch hole in the center of the playing card then use a razor blade to cut a slit in the fold at the bottom of a #4 coin envelope which is 3"(4 1/2" in size. Do not cut the slit on either side of the fold, but along the fold itself. You will also need to have a large needle threaded with about a yard of light yarn.

ROUTINE: 1. Show the card, put it into the envelope, and seal it shut.
2. Hold the envelope in your left hand, with the flap at the top and the face toward your audience, and as your right hand reaches for the needle and yarn, squeeze the sides of the envelope. The card should then slide down and stop against your curled little finger.
3. Place the point of the needle on your side of the envelope and just above the top edge of the card, pushing it through. Pull on the yarn until half of it is on each side of the envelope and give both ends to someone to hold.
4. Bring your right hand behind the envelope so your thumb is at the bottom and your fingers on the flap end. As you bring the envelope down to a horizontal position, push the card back up into the envelope. If you move your hand toward the ends of the yarn at the same time, the card will move quite easily with the yarn running around its upper end.
5. Show both sides of the envelope so your audience can see the yarn going through it.
6. Pick up a pair of scissors and cut off the bottom end of the envelope so you get rid of the slit end.
7. Reach into the envelope, hold the end of the card, and as you pull it out of the envelope, move the envelope along the yarn so you get rid of the extra yarn outside the envelope at the same time.

HOUDINI CARD UNCOVERED

EFFECT: You show 10 to 12 playing cards, all of which have a hole punched near one end. One of the cards is freely selected by a spectator, memorized, and then returned to the packet, which is cut a couple of times. A heavy string is now threaded through the holes in the cards, the threaded packet given to the spectator to hold, and you hold the two ends of the string. The spectator names his card, you pull on the string, and the threaded packet comes away from his fingers leaving him holding only his selected card.

ONE, TWO, THREE, MAGIC!

PROPS NEEDED: 10 to 12 old playing cards, a paper punch, a length of heavy twine

SECRET: The trick is dependent on a secret card move called The Glide and even though it is very easy to do, you should practice it until it's done smoothly and invisibly.

PREPARATION: Remove a dozen cards from an old deck and get a paper punch. Punch a hole in one card 3/4" from one end and then use that card as a template to punch a hole in each of the other cards in exactly the same place. You only need a hole in one end of each card. Now get a piece of heavy string about 24" long and dip each end into some glue to stiffen it. Allow it to dry thoroughly.

Put one end of the string through the holes in all the cards, bring the two ends together, and tie a loose knot in them to keep everything together.

ROUTINE: 1. Remove the string from the cards, drop it on the table, and spread the cards between your hands so someone can take one.

2. Separate the cards near the center of the spread for the return of the memorized card and as you close the packet, slip just the ball of the tip of your left little finger under the right edge of the selected card. Now, when the packet is closed, there is an opening under the selected card in the center of the packet and if you keep the outer end  of the packet closed, no one can see it. To make sure, keep the left edge of the packet in the crotch of your left thumb.

3. Bring your right hand on top of the packet so your thumb is at the inner end and your fingers at the outer end and with your left thumb, riffle some cards off the bottom of the packet, pull them away with your left hand, and put them on top.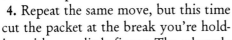

4. Repeat the same move, but this time cut the packet at the break you're holding with your little finger. The selected card will now be on the bottom of the packet.

5. Turn the packet so you hold it face down in your left hand, with your fingers on one long edge and your thumb on the opposite side and with your palm toward the floor. The packet is held so the holes in the cards are at the outer end.

6. As you use your right hand at the outer end of the packet to square it, your left two middle fingers pull the bottom card away from the outer end of the packet. Pull it far enough that it clears the holes punched in the other cards. Your left fingers create a screen to hide the end of the card extending from the packet as you pick up the string with your right hand.

7. Drop one end of the string down through the hole in the packet, pull to bring the two ends together, and then hold the string in place as your right fingers take the threaded end of the packet.

8. At the same time, push the packet to your left until it stops against your left little finger and the selected card is now even with the other cards.

9. Pull the packet from your left hand, squaring it as you do so, and have the person who selected the card take the other end of the cards. They are to hold the packet with the tips of their fingers on the bottom of the packet and their thumb on top.

10. Wrap the ends of the string once around your finger, snap the fingers of your other hand, and pull the packet out of their hand. They will be left holding their selected card.

IMPORTANT POINTS: Practice the two moves (making and holding the break in the center of the packet and gliding the bottom card of the packet) until you can do them smoothly so they can't be seen by your audience. Also, you'll notice that when you push the selected card square with the threaded packet that everything looks fair, even if you look into the hole in the cards.

THE VANISHING COIN

EFFECT: After putting a dime into your hand you close your fingers over it. When you open your hand again, the coin is gone and you reproduce it from your pocket.

PROPS NEEDED: Two dimes, a piece of soft soap or soft wax or plastic adhesive

PREPARATION: You need a spot of soft soap or a plastic adhesive like Stik-Tac on the nail of your right ring finger. You also need two dimes in your left pocket.

ROUTINE: 1. Reach into your left pocket and remove one of the dimes as you flatten out your right hand palm up and with your fingers spread.

2. Put the dime in the center of the palm of your right hand, and close your fingers as you turn your hand over.

ONE, TWO, THREE, MAGIC!

3. Wait for a couple of seconds to give yourself time to push the dime against your fingernail, snap your left fingers, then start to open your right hand and turn it over. Time it so no one can see the dime sticking to your fingernail and finish with your hand palm up and empty.

4. At the same time, your left hand goes into your pocket to bring out the duplicate dime and your right hand then drops to your side so your thumb can pull the dime off your fingernail.

EGYPTIAN CARD MYSTERY

EFFECT: Someone shuffles a deck and then hands it to you behind your back. Standing so everyone can see the bottom card of the pack, you rub a finger over the face of the card and then name its color. Tossing that card aside, you repeat the same for the next five or six cards, correctly naming the color of each card.
PROPS NEEDED: A deck of cards
SECRET: You need a secret friend who is standing fairly near you. All the friend has to do is say something, anything, out loud whenever a red card comes into view on the bottom of the deck. One or two words are enough for you to recognize your friend's voice and know that the present card is red. If you don't hear your friend's voice, then you know that the card is black.

THE MYSTERY MATCH

EFFECT: You loosely fold a handkerchief around a wooden match and then have someone break the match. When the cloth is opened up, the match is still in one piece.
PROPS NEEDED: A matchbox full of matches, a handkerchief
PREPARATION: You need to find a handkerchief with a flat, wide hem rather than a small rolled one. Carefully slide a match into the hem through the opening in one corner and push it until it's about an inch away from the corner. Have two or three other matches in your pocket.

ROUTINE: 1. Lay the handkerchief out flat on the table and drop a match onto the center. Pick up the corner of the hank that has the hidden match near it and cover the loose match.

2. Keep your eye on where the match that is in the hem is located as you put the other corners into the center of the hank.

3. Pick up the bundle of cloth in one hand, find the hidden match with the other hand, and give that match to someone.

4. "Break the match," you tell them. "Fine, now break it the other way so we definitely have two separate pieces. The handkerchief is folded around them so we won't lose them when I open it up."

5. When the match is broken, you say, "Watch!" and you open the handkerchief to show an unbroken match. As they inspect the match, you can shake out the handkerchief and put it back into your pocket.

MAKING A KNOT

EFFECT: Laying a handkerchief on the table, you challenge anyone to tie a knot in it without letting go of either end. When they confess that they can't, you show them how easy it is.

PROPS NEEDED: A handkerchief

SECRET: Cross your arms, pick up one corner in one hand and lean down so your other hand can pick up the other end. Pull on the two ends as you uncross your arms and you'll tie a knot in the center.

HOUDINI'S SHEARS

EFFECT: A pair of scissors is tied to the end of a length of rope or heavy string and you challenge anyone to remove the scissors without using the ends of the cord.

PROPS NEEDED: A pair of scissors, a length of cord or light rope about three feet long.

ROUTINE: 1. To tie the scissors onto the cord, bring the two ends of the cord together, and hold the cord by the loop in the center.

2. Push the loop away from you through the bottom loop of the handles of the scissors so about two inches are on the other side.

3. Open the scissors slightly, push the two ends of the cord up through the loop of the cord, and pull the knot tight around the loop of the handle.

4. Put the two ends of the cord on the other side of the scissors (away from you) and pull them toward you through the upper loop of the handles.

5. Pull the knot tight, close the scissors, and give the ends of the cord to someone to hold.

6. Challenge anyone to remove the scissors from the cord without using the ends of the cord.

7. When you're finally asked to show how it can be done, take center of the loop of cord, and pull it up the doubled cord and through the upper loop of the handles, making sure that you don't twist the cord. Keep pulling until you have a loop of rope equal to the length of the scissors.

8. Bring the center of the loop out and over the tips of the blades and back towards the handles.

9. Put the loop over the ends of the handles and pull the cord free of the scissors.

IMPORTANT POINT: You definitely have to practice this trick a few times to make sure that you know how to keep the cord straight as you manipulate it around the scissors.

THROUGH AND OVER

EFFECT: This is a great trick when you see someone who's wearing a vest.

Take a piece of heavy cord about six feet long and tie the two ends together. Have the person wearing the vest put one hand through the loop and then put their thumb of that hand into a vest pocket. The challenge is to remove the cord without untying it, cutting it, or taking the person's hand away from the vest.

PROPS NEEDED: A length of cord six feet long, someone who is wearing a vest

SECRET: It's all in the way you manipulate the cord through the armholes of the vest.

ROUTINE: 1. Take the upper end of the loop of cord, the one that's hanging on the person's arm, and push it through the armhole of the vest, up over their head, and out the opposite armhole.

2. The hand of that arm now goes through the loop, the end of the loop goes back into the armhole of the vest, and you can now pull the loop down under the vest to their feet so they can step free of the cord.

IMPORTANT POINTS: If the person is larger or taller than average, then you will need a longer cord, probably about eight feet long before you tie it into a loop.

Their hand, the one on the arm that has the loop in the beginning, has to be anchored to the vest. This means that they put their thumb into a vest pocket, or between two buttons on the front of the vest. They may NOT put their hand on their hip or in their pants pocket.

DELAND'S MIND READING TRICK
(Theodore L. DeLand)

EFFECT: Giving someone a piece of paper and a pencil, you point to someone else and tell them to think of any playing card. After you've left the room, the one spectator names the card and the second person writes the name of that card on the paper, folds it up, and puts it on the table. After this is done, you come back into the room, touch the folded paper with your little finger, and correctly name the card.

PROPS NEEDED: A sheet of note paper A pencil A table

SECRET: This is another trick where you need a secret friend, and this is the person you give the paper and pencil to. Ahead of time the two of you have agreed about which table you're going to use, and which door you will use in leaving and returning to the room.

The table is mentally divided in sections, as you, the magician, will be looking at it. It's divided into four sections by imaginary lines running from corner to corner, and each section represents one of the four suits. There is also an imaginary circle in the center of the table that is considered like a clock dial, and that will be used as a value indicator.

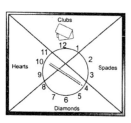

ROUTINE: For the purposes of explanation, we will suppose that the card named will be the Four of Clubs.

1. Hand the piece of paper and the pencil to your fellow conspirator then point to someone else who is to name a card after you leave the

room. Explain that the card is to be written on the paper, the paper folded twice so the writing can't be read, and then to be put on the table.
2. Leave the room.
3. When a card is named, your confederate writes the name on the paper, lets everyone see it, and then folds up the paper.
4. He places the folded note in the section of the tabletop that denotes the suit of the selected card. The pencil is then put in the center of the table, but with the point aimed at the part of the clock dial that represents the value of the card; the Jack is represented by 11 and the Queen by 12. If the card is a King, he puts the pencil on top of the folded paper. If someone has named the Joker, he then puts the pencil in his pocket and the note anywhere on the table.
5. You come back into the room, and as you put one of your little fingers on top of the note, you take in the information coded to you by your friend. Name the card, and then take a bow for doing a card trick without using a deck of cards.

THE AFGHAN BANDS

EFFECT: Showing a large circle of cloth or paper, you take a pair of scissors and cut along its length to make two loops. You then cut one of those hoops as well, but it turns out to be two rings that are linked. When the second loop is cut it becomes one large circle twice the size of the original.
PROPS NEEDED: A length of cotton, cambric, or paper, 4" wide by 48" long, a gluestick, scissors
SECRET: Unknown to the audience there are twists in the band.
PREPARATION: Flatten out the cotton strip and then bring the two ends of the strip together (making sure that the strip doesn't get twisted) and in each end make three cuts so you now have four tabs 1"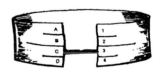
wide and about 3" long. Consider the tabs on the left side as A, B, C, and D, and the tabs on the other end as 1, 2, 3, and 4. Match the two ends so the tabs are touching each other.
   Pick up A and B, give them a half-twist and glue each of them to 1 and 2 so that A goes on 2 and B goes on 1. Take the bottom two tabs, C and D, give them a full twist, and glue them to the opposite tabs so

that C goes on 3 and D goes on 4.

Double up the loop, but remember where those cut tabs are in the resulting bundle.

If you have used cotton or cambric to make your prop, you won't need scissors for the routine, as you'll be able to easily tear the rings apart.

ROUTINE: 1. Open up the bundle, hold the part that has the glued tabs in your left hand, and pick up the scissors. Insert the scissors in the middle cut (between B and C), and cut along the length of the loop. When you finish you will have two separate loops.

2. Show the two separate loops and put one over your left arm. Hold the other one in your left hand at the tabs and cut this loop down the center. When you finish you have either two linked loops or one giant circle.

3. When you cut the loop that you had over your arm, you will have a giant circle or two linked loops.

IMPORTANT POINT: If you want to know which loop will become the two linked loops, use a pen to mark tabs A and B with a 2 after you glue them to the other tabs. That will mean two loops and the unmarked tabs will give you the large circle.

THE CUPS & BALLS

This trick, as we told you in the first chapter, is the oldest trick in the world and every magician has his favorite routine. Once you understand the moves and psychology of the trick, you can start working out your own routine so it will be different from everyone else's.

EFFECT: Three cups and three balls are put on the table in two straight lines, with the balls in front of the cups. A ball is put on top of one cup, the other two cups are put on top, the cups are tapped, and when lifted, the ball is now on the table. This is repeated with the other two balls so that all three balls finish together on the table.

Now one ball is put under each cup, the two outside cups are tapped, and those balls vanish to appear under the center cup with its ball.

PROPS NEEDED: Three cups without handles, that look exactly alike, and that will nest one inside another. When nested there must be room

ONE, TWO, THREE, MAGIC!

between the bottoms of the cups for a hidden ball. The cups can be metal, ceramic, wood, or even paper cups, as long as all of the requirements are fulfilled.

There are four balls, and they should be soft (sponge or foam rubber are very good) and about a half inch to three-quarters of an inch in diameter. You can also use the little fuzzy balls from ball fringe that you can buy in a craft or fabric store.

SECRET: An extra, hidden ball and they way you handle the cups.

PREPARATION: First of all, put a ball inside a cup, then nest one of the other cups on the inside of that cup, and nest both of those cups inside the third one. The ball is now inside the middle cup.

Hold the cups mouth up and consider them numbered from bottom to top as 1, 2, and 3. Whenever the cups are nested together in your left hand in this position, they have those numbers. In other words, the cups don't keep the same numbers through the routine, only when you're holding them nested mouth upwards in your left hand.

The table in front of you has three imaginary spots where you will put the cups, usually one cup to each spot. These spots are about 4" apart and will always be considered as A, B, and C from left to right.

To start the routine, have a ball in the middle cup and the other three balls in cup 3.

ROUTINE: 1. Roll the three balls out onto the table, and then hold the cups mouth upwards in your left hand as your right hand puts one ball in front of each of the spaces on the table: A, B, and C.
2. Your right hand comes over, pulls cup 1 down away from the other two, and sets it in place at

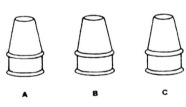

A, turning the cup upside down as you do so. The cup is now mouth downwards on the table and behind the ball at that position.
3. Take cup 2 and place it upside down on B and behind its ball. Do this naturally and with the same deliberate speed as when you handled cup 1 and the ball inside the cup will stay inside the cup.
4. Take cup 3 and put it upside down on C, behind that ball.
5. Pick up ball B and put it on the bottom of cup B.
6. Pick up cup C and put it over the ball on B, then put cup A on top of the other two cups.
7. Tap the bottom of the top cup.
8. Lift all three cups to show a ball on the table then place the cup

mouth up in your left hand.

9. Again put cup 1 on space A and behind the ball there.
10. Put cup 2 on top of the ball at B.
11. Put cup 3 at C and behind that ball.
12. Pick up the ball at A, put it on the cup at B, and then put the other two cups on top (move #5).
13. Tap the bottom of the top cup.
14. Lift all three cups to show that there are now two balls on the table and put the cups into your left hand.
15. Repeat moves 8 through 10 then put the ball at C on top of cup B.
16. Put the other two cups on top, tap the bottom of the cups, and lift them to show three balls on the table. Put the three cups into your left hand.
17. With your right hand, again put a ball at each of the three spots.
18. Again put a cup at each spot, one behind each ball. You again have a secret ball under the cup at B.
19. With your left hand, tip the top of the cup at A slightly backward (keeping the back edge of the cup on the table) and with the tips of your right fingers pretend to push ball A under the cup. Instead, you keep the ball at your fingertips, but hidden from your audience, and drop the cup down onto an empty space. Say, "One."
20. Your left hand tips cup B backwards and your right fingers push ball B along with the hidden ball under the cup. Say, "Two."
21. Tip back the cup at C, apparently push ball C underneath, but keep it in your fingers as you let the cup back down onto the table. Say, "Three."
22. As you ask your audience to watch the three cups closely, you roll the hidden ball so it is clipped between your middle and ring fingers just below the first joint.
23. Pick up the cup at A so everyone can see that that ball is gone and put the mouth of the cup into your right fingertips. As your left hand continues on toward cup C, your right hand turns slightly so the ball can secretly drop straight down into the cup. Your left hand picks up cup C and your right hand drops its cup into the cup in your left hand.
24. Your right hand picks up cup B to show all three balls on the table and then drops that cup into the other two.
25. Drop the three balls into the mouth of cup 3 and you're all set for the next time you do the trick.

IMPORTANT POINTS: Again, the strength of this basic routine is based on a steady 1-2-3 tempo. Don't hurry through it as you want your audience to understand what you're doing at all stages, but you don't want to go so slowly that they get ahead of you and figure out what you're going to do.

Although this routine doesn't take any sleight of hand, it looks like it does. So don't tell anyone that it's simple, let the audience draw their own conclusions about the amount of your skill.

Later, as you meet other magicians and read more books on magic, you'll come across other routines with the Cups & Balls. Watch them closely, decide which ones you would like to do, and then learn them. Soon you'll have two or three different routines and they will probably be of different levels of sleight of hand skill.

Bibliography

BRANDON, Ruth - *The Life and Many Deaths of Harry Houdini*, Random House, New York, 1993.

CHRISTOPHER, Milbourne - *The Illustrated History of Magic*, Thomas Y. Crowell, New York, 1973.
- *Panorama of Magic*, Dover Publications, New York, 1962.

COOKSEY, Chas. F. - *Who was King Arthur?*, W. Mate and Sons, Ltd., Southampton, England, n.d.

DUMAS, François Ribadeau - *Cagliostro*, Orion Press, New York, 1967.

Encyclopedia Britannica - Vol. 20, Encyclopedia Britannica, Inc., Chicago, 1963.

FECHNER, Christian - *Bibliographie de la Prestidigitation Française et des Arts annexes*, Editions F.C.F., Boulogne, France, 1994.

GODWIN, William - *Lives of the Necromancers*, Frederick J. Mason, London, 1834.

HALL, Manly P. - *The Secret Teachings of All Ages*, Philosophical Research Society, Inc., Los Angeles, 1973.

Houdini's Book of Magic and Party Pastimes, Stoll & Edwards Co., Inc., New York, 1927.

JAY, Ricky - *Learned Pigs & Fireproof Women*, Villard Books, New York, 1987.

Man, Myth & Magic, Vols. 3, 13, & 20, Marshall Cavendish Corp., New York, 1970.

MORLEY, Henry - *Memoirs of Bartholomew Fair*, George Routledge and Sons, Ltd., London, 1892.

RANDI, James - *Conjuring*, St. Martin's Press, New York, 1992.

SILVERMAN, Kenneth - *HOUDINI!!!*, HarperCollins, New York, 1996.

SITWELL, Edith - *English Eccentrics*, The Folio Society, London, 1996.

SMITH, H. Adrian - *Books at Brown*, Friends of the Library of Brown University, Providence RI, 1987.

TARBELL, Harlan - *Tarbell Course in Magic*, Vol. 1, Louis Tannen, New York, 1941.

TOOLE-STOTT, Raymond - A Bibliography of English Conjuring 1581- 1876, Harpur & Sons, Derby, England, 1976.

WHALEY, Bart - Who's Who in Magic, Jeff Busby Magic, Inc., Wallace ID, 1991.

MORE TO COME...

This is the first of two volume work created to teach you the secrets of performing magic. The books are designed so you can learn to perform tricks that will delight and amaze your family, your friends and business associates. Return to the shop where you bought this book and ask the clerk about volume 2 or contact us toll free at 877-346-4946 or go to houdini.com.

HARRY HOUDINI'S
School of Magic.

INVENTOR, ORIGINATOR AND
Manufacturing :: Magician.
221 E. 69th Street,
NEW YORK CITY.
Send Money in Any Safe Way.

Second Sight.

Lay 3 cards on table, and leave room, and allow someone to touch a card, you on entering can walk right over to the cards and tell which was touched. Secret: Have a friend place a toothpick in his mouth and if the center card is touched have pick in center of mouth, and if end card was touched have pick in end of mouth. This is very clever. Try it.

Change a glass of Ink into Water.

Fill glass with water, and place black silk around glass (inside) and it will look like ink; now cover it with handkerchief and pull silk out and you have water.

1   How to Hypnotize any Animal.

This is very easy to do.   Secret, $1.00.

2 Fortune Telling, as worked by Gipsies.

The only real and sure method. With this secret you can tell anyone's past, present and future just as readily as the best medium in the world. Secret, $2.50.

3 Letter Reading or Clairvoyance.

How to read questions inside of envelope without opening the envelope, and to show that you have read it correctly, you tear it open and hand it to audience to read.   Secret, $1.00.

4   Fortune Telling Cards.

If you desire to tell fortunes with cards, I have marked the face of cards so that you can tell any one's fortune by reading the cards. Every card is marked what it represents. Price, per pack, 75c. A list of what the cards mean,   30c.

5   How to walk a Ladder of Keen Edged Swords.

Anyone can do it possessing secret. Secret and explanations, $1.00.

6   Barrel Mystery.

An ordinary 58 gallon cask, inspected by committee, who lock, strap and seal performer up, but who can free himself at will. Price, complete, $25.00. Secret, plans, etc., $5.00.

7   The Maniac's Strategy.

My own INVENTION and Idea.

While visiting St. John, N. B., in 1896 I visited the insane asylum and under the care of Dr. Steenes, Physician of Insane, I was shown a bed called a crib, from which a prisoner, a maniac, in some unaccountable way released himself and escaped handcuffed and manacled. I made a study of the crib, and mounted it. I claim it to be the strongest single act before the public. Detection is impossible. Complete, with crib, cabinet, handcuffs, leg irons and all necessary apparatus, $100.00 Also full story of escape by prisoner. Secret, plans, etc., $10.00. This cannot be had elsewhere. Fine for medium, as none of the apparatus is faked.

The Wonderful Hat.

Upon a table place three pieces of bread, or any other eatable substance, at a little distance from each other, and cover each with a hat; take up the first hat, and, removing the bread put it into your mouth, letting the company see that you swallowed it; then raise the second hat, and eat the bread which is under that hat; then proceed to the third hat in the same manner. Having eaten the three pieces, ask any person in the company to choose which hat he would like the three pieces of bread to be under, and when he has made his choice of one of the hats, put it on your head, and ask him if he does not think they are under it.

Genuine Black Art.

Stick a pin in crown of silk hat and leave half-inch stick out; then request some one to extract with teeth only. Tell him this is black art. You have blackened the top of hat beforehand, and

HARRY HOUDINI'S
School of Magic.

INVENTOR, ORIGINATOR AND
Manufacturing :: Magician.
221 E. 69th Street,
NEW YORK CITY.
Send Money in Any Safe Way.

Color block held between fingers, change color is often as desired, 50 cents.

Cards change from all picture to all spots, or all black to all red, 12 cents.

20 Rising Cards.

How to make cards rise out of deck placed into a tumbler. Secret and all directions, 75 cents.

21 Traveling Money.

A borrowed and marked dime or quarter found in center of ball of wool. Apparatus and full secret, 50 cents.

22 Marked Cards.

In magic they are useful in a hundred ways. In poker you can call down "bluffs," raise out weak hands and always win. A little study makes you an expert, Per pack, $1.50.

23 The Turning Cards.

A card rises from the pack with back instead of face toward the audience, turns around at command in full sight of audience. A very pretty trick and easy. Price, 50 cents.

24 Muchoir du Diable or the Demon Handkerchief.

Indispensable to every conjuror. Watches, rings, coins and any articles placed under this handkerchief instantly disappear, although the handkerchief is thoroughly shaken and shown to the audience each time. Very superior make. Price, post free, 75 cents. Secret, 25 cents.

25 The Torn Card,

A fine trick. You can tear the corner off this card and by blowing the corner appears in its place. Price, 35 cents. Secret, 10 cents.

With which many wonderful tricks can be done without practice. Price, 75 cents.

A card which becomes smaller or larger, 10c.

Any one having one of these packs can tell at once what card is chosen by the audience; 30 cents.

Borrowed coin, dances and answers questions. Secret only needed, 25 cents.

Invisible hen, which lays eggs in handkerchief, which are placed in hat and then vanish. Apparatus, complete, 75c. Secret, 25c.

26 The Wonderful Rattle Box.

A most excellent trick. Indispensable to a conjuror. A marked coin is borrowed and placed in the box. The coin is heard to rattle in the box, when suddenly the sound ceases and the coin is found at the far end of the room, or in a gentleman's pocket, the box being shown quite empty. Price, post free, 50c. Secret, 20c.

Spanish Pillory Act. Secret, $1.00.

Lady—from an envelope. Secret, 50c.

Two of my easy methods of silent second sight, blackboard work; requires no practice. Both methods, $1.00.

Any six 50c secrets, $1.25.

Any seven $1.00 secrets, $6.25.

$20.00 worth of secrets, $12.50.

Special prices for apparatus by the quantity.

Magicians' flowers that expand, per dozen, 50c; 50 for $2.00; 100 for $3.75.

27 New Mysterious Coin.

The greatest coin trick in existence, and is the invention of the celebrated A. Roterberg, of Chicago, the man that always has something new.

Any coin is borrowed and held with tips of fingers; it vanishes; both hands shown empty; coin reappears. Can be repeated as often as desired. The hands do not come near the body. No palming; no rubber or string used; no sleeve work. A fine pocket trick. Easy. Price, 50c; secret, 20c.

To cut a piece out of center of borrowed handkerchief and restore it in full view of the audience. New. Any handkerchief used. Price, 75 cents; secret, 25c.

28 Spirit Mediums.

Lessons given in Rope Tying, Fantasmagoria, etc. Mediums instructed personally or by mail. Valuable information for any one giving spiritualistic entertainments. Terms on application.

29 Half-Dollar Wand.

It is not thicker than your finger, and any amount of half dollars are caught on end of same. Price, $4.00 to $8.00, according to finish. Secret, 25c.

30 Cremation.

The best and easiest and simplest way of performing this beautiful illusion. Full secret, with drawings, $1.50.

31 Blood Writing on the Arm.

Any word written on a paper and put in an

HARRY HOUDINI'S
School of Magic.

INVENTOR, ORIGINATOR AND

Manufacturing :: Magician.

221 E. 69th Street,
NEW YORK CITY.

Send Money in Any Safe Way.

Red, White and Blue.

Have a flag concealed on your table; take 8 pieces of tissue paper and lay flag under paper; when you pick up paper also pick up flag and roll paper together and unfold flag, keeping paper behind flag.

The Jesse James Tape Trick.

Have two pieces of braid, string or ribbon fastened together in center, separate the ends and the ribbons will be like two letter VV's tied like this > <; tie around neck and pull ends.

Magnetic Stick.

Take piece fine wood and put a pin at bottom, point portruding, and by placing it into palm of hand it will cause stick to rise.

Magic Card.

Have a piece of thread tied to your vest button and on end of thread have a pellet of wax; spread cards on table and slyly put wax on card and whistle, as you whistle move away and card will follow you, then tear off wax and hand the card for inspection

10   The Magic Stew Pan.

The performer shows to the company a stew pan, which can be examined. He then takes several eggs and breaks them in the pan, pours over them spirits of wine, which he lights to cook the eggs; then placing the cover on the "stew pan," he commands the cooked eggs to change into live doves or pigeons. The cover is lifted up, and inside the stew pan is found the two birds, alive. The birds are taken out and shown to the company. This effective trick can be performed with ease, and will cause great astonishment. Price, $2.00.

11   Jumping Card

A selected card jumps from the pack at command. Price, 10 cents.

12   The Marvelous Turning Card

A card having risen from the pack with the back instead of the face towards the audience, turns around at command in full sight of the audience, the performer standing at a distance from the same. Price, 75 cents. Good for rising card trick. Secret, 20 cents.

13   The Magic Envelope

Any card, coin or picture put in this envelope changes into any other desired article or vanishes altogether. Price, 10 cents.

You Are Never Too Old to Learn!
LEARN TO BE ENTERTAINING!

If you cannot sing or dance or tell a funny story and you want to entertain your company, amuse them with a few Magic Tricks. I will send you the following tricks for $2.50:

1. THE WONDERFUL EGG BAG, with which you cause an egg to vanish and appear at will.
2. THE DEVIL'S HANDKERCHIEF.—A watch, egg, coin or any object lain in handkerchief disappears immediately.
3. THE MYSTERIOUS CHANGING ENVELOPE.
4. WONDERFUL CHANGING CARD.—Changes three times while held in one hand without covering.
5. TORN CORNER CARD.—To tear a corner off a card and restore it right before the very eyes.
6. SPIRIT CARD.—Which becomes larger or smaller.
7. CHANGING COLOR CUBES.—A wonderful pocket trick. A pair of cubes color while being held in hand.

These tricks require no practice, and can be done anywhere by any one possessing the apparatus, which I send with full instructions. Best $2.50 you may ever spend.

HARRY HOUDINI, 221 E. 69th Street, New York City.

Send 10c. for a Large Book

CONTAINING

Songs, Recitations, Puzzles, Games, Parlor Magic, Experiments, Money Making Secrets, Recipes, Jokes, Riddles, Pictures, 25 Favorite Actresses, Presidents of the United States, Etc., Etc.

THE BEST BOOK FOR THE MONEY EVER PUBLISHED

THIS BOOK IS CALLED

The Premium Budget.

SEND 10c. FOR IT.

HOUDINI'S SCHOOL OF MAGIC,

221 E. 69th Street, New York City.

HARRY HOUDINI'S
School of Magic.

INVENTOR, ORIGINATOR AND
Manufacturing :: Magician.
221 E. 69th Street,
NEW YORK CITY.
Send Money in Any Safe Way.

14   Vanishing Cage and Bird.

A cage containing a bird vanishes in performer's hands without being covered in any way. Price of cage from $2 to $8, according to finish Secret. 25 cents.

15   Card Sword.

Three selected cards are put in pack and shuffled, and pack is thrown in air, and as they fall the performer catches the three selected cards on point of sword. Price of sword complete, from $3.00 to $8.00, according to finish.

Secret for Catching—Chosen cards on any sword. Price, 50 cents.

16   Reading Cards Blindfolded.

Performer being blindfolded, and on any pack of cards being placed in his hands, he at once proceeds to name each one in regular order, and allows cards to be shuffled at any time. A most excellent trick, not to be had elsewhere. Price, $1.00.

Punch and Judy Squeakers, with instructions for using. Price, 10 cents.

Fine Book on Card Tricks. Price, 25 cents.

The Magical Knot.

This is a very amusing trick. It consists simply in tying one knot with two ends of a handkerchief, and by apparently pulling the ends

FIG. 5.

untying them again. It is done in this manner. Take the two ends of the handkerchief, one in each hand, th ends dropping from the inside of your hands. You simply tie a single knot, when you will find your hands and the handkerchief in the position as represented in Fig. 5. Now instead of pulling the ends C and D you grasp that part of the handkerchief marked B with the thumb and forefinger, dropping the end D, a d pulling upon the end C and the B, when you will find that in A, end of tying you always unloose the knot. All this shall be d one as quickly as possible to prevent detection. Examine the engraving closely and you will more readily understand the recreation.

32   Magic Blackboard.

A skeleton is drawn on a blackboard with a piece of chalk, and at command the figure drawn on board with chalk will dance and keep time with music. This is the latest, and most mysterious and humorous trick out, and always sure of big applause. Very easy to do. Full secret. price, $1.00.

33   The Handkerchief and Candle.

A handkerchief and a candle are given for examination; performer vanishes handkerchief from his hands which are shown empty, and goes to candle where he produces handkerchief from the flame. A pretty trick, and easy. Price, $1.50. Secret, 25c.

34   The Mysterious Card Ladle.

A beautiful japanned ladle is shown, and a piece of paper is given to one of the audience, and he is asked to write his name on it; it is then placed in the ladle and burnt, the ashes being carefully kept in the ladle, but at the word of command the ashes vanish, and the piece of paper with the name on is found perfectly uninjured. Price, complete best make, $2; secret, 50c.

FREE!   FREE!

Parlor Magic, a Book containing directions for performing over one hundred amusing tricks in Magic and Legerdemain, with 121 illustrations. Free with every $2.00 purchase.

I Buy, Sell and Exchange Books
ON ALL SUBJECTS.

Mesmerism, Spiritualism, Magic in all its Branches. Books on all Mysteries, Riddles, Puzzles, Etc., Etc.

Write for anything you want, enclose stamp.